Freedom from Darkness

* 85 =

* 177 - 181

Freedom from Darkness

Rev. Angelo Del Zotto
with
Diane Roblin Lee

ISBN   1-896213-03-0

Copyright 1995 - Reverend Angelo Del Zotto

Published by
PRAISE A / V PUBLISHING
R.R. #2, Woodville, Ontario, Canada K0M 2T0

Front Cover Photo - J.P. Stewart Kaleidosculpture
Rear Cover Photo - Warren Lee
Praise Audio Visual, Woodville, Ontario, K0M 2T0

All stories recorded in this book are true.
The actual names and locations involved have been
changed to protect identities.

All Scripture quotations are taken from the
New International Version unless otherwise specified.
The NIV Study Bible, Copyright 1985 by
The Zondervan Corporation
Grand Rapids, Michigan

Printed in Canada.

Dedicated
to
the hundreds of precious people who dared to
expose their internal struggles to us in their search
for freedom from the darkness which crippled their
lives. We thank God for the lessons He taught us as
He set them free in accordance with His Word.
Seeing these dear people, in turn, leading others
from darkness into light is overwhelmingly
wonderful to us.

CONTENTS

FOREWORD

For years, when I heard the word, "deliverance", it made me cringe. My ignorance and fear of the subject caused me to avoid it completely. I felt no desire to be involved with those who seemed to be able to find a demon under every rock in their deliverance ministries. I still avoid those types of ministries.

However, through my years of pastoring, I have discovered that nothing will cause a pastor to evaluate his theology and pull his head out of the sand any faster than coming in contact with a person who is in desperate need of deliverance.

We can dance around the semantics of this thing until Jesus comes back, but let's face it, the sin of mankind has put shackles around his hands and feet from which he cannot free himself. He needs a Power greater than himself.

This book proclaims that Power and gives practical advice for the conflict that Paul talked about in Ephesians Six.

Along with scores of other people, I have been encouraging Angelo for several years to write a practical book on deliverance that will help those who minister to hurting people. Now he has done just that. The author is not a person who has no experience in this area, but is a man of incredible sensitivity and gentleness whose years of working fearlessly in this field highly qualify him to give leadership.

I have had the unique opportunity to sit in on numerous counselling sessions with Angelo and have watched as people's lives were dramatically changed and they were set free. The full effects can be expressed only by those individuals who received loving ministry and were led out of their darkness into freedom. The ministry of Jesus, according to the Scriptures, was one of imparting deliverance to those with whom He came into contact. His famous reading of the Scriptures in the Synagogue of Nazareth proclaimed what He had come to the world to do. He read with confidence the words of the Old Testament prophets concerning the ministry of Messiah and attributed them to Himself.

His ministry was to preach good news to the poor, to proclaim freedom to the prisoners, the recovery of sight to the blind, to release those oppressed and to proclaim the year of the Lord's favour. It can all be summed up in one glorious word - freedom.

This freedom, won for us through Christ's message, sacrificial death and resurrection, has to become a reality in our everyday lives.

This volume proclaims freedom. It encourages those who are believers to begin to walk like free people and to truly realize that He who lives within them is indeed greater than he that is in the world. It encourages those who minister to carry on Christ's ministry of imparting freedom. It encourages those who are in bondage with the message that they really can find Freedom from Darkness.

Reverend Dean Bursey
Emmanuel Pentecostal Church
Port Perry, Ontario, Canada

INTRODUCTION

This book must begin on a very personal note. It has been an almost impossible project to commence. I had planned to be writing at my computer by the end of July but as I gaze out the window, the slate grey skies of early November hang ominously over the ragged fall fields.

No matter. I'm finally able to begin.

For a long time - several years, I have struggled to overcome the guilt of past difficulties, the pain of raising a child who was molested by someone we trusted implicitly, the sometimes overwhelming stresses of running a family business, the tension of gently steering a young son and his even younger wife with their three babies through the rapids of those early years of marriage, all the while writing books and scripts, managing our home, caring for parents with Alzheimer's and dealing with the death of my father. I turned to food for comfort and my weight crept up over two hundred pounds.

It all added up to a big fat depression. On the surface, I appeared to cope with everything, but I never really felt happy. Every day meant another trudge around the mountain without any personal enjoyment. Everything was a chore. My smiles were forced and were always worn for the calculated comfort of others, seldom a reflection of my heart. Every cell of my being seemed to be pervaded by a heavy, drooping sadness.

I prayed morsels of prayers through a thick fog of heavy grey oppression, but my words seemed to sit lifelessly on the air in front of my mouth, without going anywhere. I was too despondent to read the Bible. Everything seemed hopeless.

I went to a doctor who prescribed Prozac. He said that

3

he could not begin to work with me until the drug began to take effect. Because my husband objected to the pharmacological approach, I did some research on Prozac and decided that he was right. The side effects of the drug could have been worse than the depression. His sensitivity to God had protected me.

I called Angelo and made an appointment with him and his wife, Carmen, for prayer. As they confronted things like unforgiveness and resentment in my heart, I desperately resisted in spite of my desire to be free. Those things were there for good reason and allowing the walls to come down would mean that I would be vulnerable again. Finally, in a wrenching act of my will, I declared my forgiveness for those toward whom I had held bitterness.

Something left. Peace gently trickled throughout my body and soul. I was free.

Now I can begin to write.

Diane Roblin Lee

THE WHOLE RECIPE

Imagine a teacher in a cooking school who has the recipe for a scrumptious chocolate cake. He advertises publicly that he is going to bake a stupendous cake every Sunday morning at 11 A.M. He invites anyone who would like to have a piece to come and participate as he instructs his students in the Sunday morning class.

Of course it sounds wonderful - free cake! All over the city on Sunday morning, people get up, dress their families and drive to the cooking school.

When they arrive, they are greeted at the door by a smiling student who shakes their hands and passes them a copy of the recipe. As they sit down at their assigned desks, they read over the list of ingredients and the baking instructions. Their mouths begin to water. They know that this is the cake they have been waiting for all of their lives. The ingredients are pure genius. The nutritional aspects of the cake alone would win an international award.

As they sit waiting for the teacher to arrive for the baking session, they look around at the others in the room. It's easy to tell the students from the visitors because the students all wear uniforms - the women have pouffy hair, frilly blouses and fake eyelashes and the men wear brown polyester suits - and almost every one of them is skinny, skinny, skinny. Why? If this cake is as good as it is supposed to be, and if it is baked over and over again, why aren't the students fat?

As the visitors contemplate this unsettling question, the teacher enters.

He approaches the podium with a flourish and welcomes one and all to his class. He asks everyone to please rise and read the recipe aloud in unison with him. Following the morning reading, he asks them all to be seated. For the next hour, he drones on about the marvellous attributes of the cake they will soon taste. He makes great promises and boasts unabashedly about his culinary skills.

Finally it is time for some action. He rereads the list of ingredients and assembles them on the counter beside the podium. He then reaches under the counter and sets a huge, filthy bowl on it. It looks as though it has never been washed since it was purchased. He proceeds to fill the filthy bowl with the marvellous ingredients. As he works, he enthusiastically tells his audience how wonderful the cake will be.

Everyone is spellbound. They are shocked that he would put all of the expensive ingredients in the slimy bowl without washing it first. However, because he is the teacher, they think that he must know what he is doing. They believe his words of promise. They can hardly wait to feel that light, buttery chocolate marvel melting in their mouths.

Finally, the ingredients have all been put in the huge, filthy bowl. According to the recipe, it is now time to mix everything together and beat it before putting it into the oven to bake.

But wait - what is the teacher doing? He's passing the bowl around to everyone!

"Here," he smiles with pride at the first student. "Have a piece of my cake!"

"No thanks," the student shakes his head in rejection of the sloppy mess in the disgusting bowl. "It made me sick last week."

"You just don't appreciate fine cake", snaps the teacher. "Here," he fawns nauseatingly at a visitor and extends the bowl in his direction, "have some of my world famous cake."

The visitor looks incredulously from the teacher to the

slop in the bowl. "You can't be serious. I came here for a piece of cake. If you think I'm going to eat out of that dirty bowl, you're crazy! That mess hasn't even been mixed, let alone beaten or baked!"

"Well of course not", The teacher asserts with pompous assurity. "When I begin to put the ingredients into this bowl, it automatically becomes clean. Every speck of garbage is instantly eliminated. And as far as the mixing is concerned, well, we don't mix our ingredients at this school. I discovered a long time ago that certain students don't like certain ingredients and I wouldn't want to offend anyone by mixing everything together."

"But it says right here, that the next step is to mix the ingredients", the visitor says, pointing at the recipe.

"Oh, don't pay any attention to that. I don't believe that it's necessary to mix anything", the teacher scoffs. "Even if I didn't have to worry about certain people taking offence at the inclusion of certain ingredients, I could have a real mess on my hands if I began to mix, you know. I hate messes."

The visitor can't believe what he's hearing. "Well, even I know that a cake has to be beaten, poured into pans and baked in an oven. This stuff you're passing us is not cake."

"Look", the teacher pretends patience. "Every ingredient in that recipe is here in this bowl. Read the list. At the top it says, 'Chocolate Cake'. Here are the ingredients. This is cake. I don't even own a set of beaters. Beating is an unnecessarily radical thing to do to ingredients. Anyway, it is important for the integrity of the ingredients that they should be allowed to retain their own identity. They're all a part of cake anyway. And as far as separate pans go, well, you can imagine the trouble I could get into by pouring unmixed ingredients into separate pans. No one would know where anything was. And baking? We like to keep this place cool. Turning on the oven would be a definite affront to our comfort zone. Here. Try my cake." He extends the bowl once more to the disgusted visitor.

The visitor pushes the bowl away and gets up to leave but before he goes, his curiosity overwhelms him. He turns to the student who rejected the bowl just before it was passed to him. "Excuse me", he says. "You obviously come here week after week. You're supposed to be a cooking school student but you obviously don't eat. Look at you. You're so skinny. Why do you keep coming back here if you know that you're not going to learn to cook properly and there's nothing here to nourish you?"

"Well, here's the way it is", the student replies with obvious embarrassment. "It's not entirely true that there's nothing here to nourish me. The ingredients are excellent. I just keep coming back, week after week, hoping that one day the teacher will wash the bowl, follow the instructions in the recipe and actually bake the cake so that we can really celebrate and enjoy the reality of it as it is supposed to be."

"You're crazy. I'm not even a student but even I know better than to settle for eating unbaked cake from a filthy bowl when I know that somewhere the reality of yummy, properly prepared, baked cake exists." He turns and walks away, leaving everyone in the room to deal with the question of whether or not to demand that the bowl be washed and the recipe be followed in its entirety.

Before people accept Christ into their hearts, they live as empty bowls lined with a layer of grunge - bodies with unredeemed souls (the soul encompasses the will, the intellect, the personality and the emotions) waiting to be filled by the Spirit of God. When Christ comes in, however, unless He is received on His terms according to His will as specified in Scripture, the bowl will not profit and the layer of grunge will not be purified.

When a person accepts Christ, he receives the righteousness (right standing) of Christ; thus as God looks at a believer, He sees him covered by a robe of righteousness. It's like the dirty bowl filled with the perfect cake which covered all of the imperfections of the container. That's how God sees redeemed man.

However, if Christians want to reach out to those around them with the love of Jesus, they need to clean out their bowls according to the provisions of the gospel. Although a beautiful cake may hide a filthy plate, the problem becomes visible once the cake is cut and an attempt is made to serve it. Until we stand redeemed before God, we are called to live in many forms of relationships on Planet Earth. Cake was meant to be shared. Acceptable sharing comes only from a clean plate.

In late 1993, I felt that the Lord was telling me to remind people of the danger of neglecting his instructions and the relationship with Him. He wanted them to feel an urgency about cleaning up their lives and becoming strong in their faith.

It bothered me that many sought the Baptism in the Holy Spirit as a goal or graduation point. Then, When they experienced the Baptism, many continued to live in bondages of one sort or another. While they were eager to partake in some of the benefits of the Lord, they seemed blinded to whole sections of the gospel. The abundant life that Jesus came to bring was like an elusive dream to them. I felt a great burden to reach people with the full gospel—the whole recipe for abundant life.

Things were changing so fast in our world that I could see the Book of Revelation being played out before my eyes. So much evil had already been unleashed on the earth that our society was almost unrecognizable from what it was even ten years before.

I felt a strong warning that unless people repented of their shallow Christianity, they would be in danger of losing their presence before the Lord. Revelation 2:4,5 burned in my heart.

"Yet I have this against you: remember the height from which you have fallen! Repent and do the things that you did at first. If you do not repent, I will come to you and remove the lamp stand from its place."

Not long after my wife, Carmen, and I became Christians, we were introduced to the reality of spiritual warfare in a very tangible way. Suffice it to say, at this point, that we were shown without a doubt that life as we had known it was a mere shadow of the reality of the awesome spiritual forces which influence and shape lives. Without an awareness of these spiritual forces and the role we play in the universe, we discovered that we are at the mercy of powers beyond the control of natural man.

Satan is gearing up for his final battle. He knows that he is going down and he wants to take everyone possible with him. He is trying to exhaust and destroy each person individually so that they will have no strength to form a united front against him.

So many Christians long for the loving relationship that they know awaits them with their Heavenly Father, but they just can't seem to get past the circumstances of their lives and the emotions that drag them down. It's as though they're slugging through four feet of thick mud with every step. They get tired and discouraged and feel like giving up. They don't recognize that they have an enemy and they are

10

under attack. Unless the full Word of God is applied to their lives, they never will get past the things that hold them back.

Unless Christians guard themselves diligently against attacks of the evil one, they will gradually fall back into their old ways and separate themselves from God. A Christian's survival and entire quality of life depends on the recognition of the fact that we do indeed have an enemy, and his battleground has always been in the minds (the souls) of men and women.

This book is about recognizing and dealing with the fact that although our lives may be filled with the essential ingredients of Christianity, our souls (our minds, personalities, thought lives, wills and emotions) need to be cleaned out and subjected to the authority of Jesus Christ.

It is about cleaning out our bowls, making sure that we include all of the ingredients of true Christianity in our lives: following and obeying God's teachings, being living witnesses of the richness of the Gospel, not allowing ourselves to be taken in by man's philosophy, being aware of truth in these days of deception and conducting ourselves as wise rather than foolish students.

It's about growing in Christ according to God's instructions rather than man's ideas and getting back to the full Gospel.

Perhaps most of all, this book is an attempt to remove the shadow of fear from Christians who apprehensively contemplate the possibility of any demonic interference in their lives or in the lives of their friends or families, and to replace it with an excitement about our abilities to live as joyous overcomers.

11

PROLOGUE

JUST THREE OF HUNDREDS OF ENCOUNTERS

Early in our ministry, God led us into circumstances where we were confronted head on with the reality of the dark kingdom. Distasteful as some of the encounters were, we knew that we could not ignore what God was showing us if we had any hope of ministering in a meaningful way to His people.

While the following stories may sound as though we've let our imaginations run a little bit wild, we declare before God that they are true. Only the names and locations have been changed to protect identities. We have not chosen our most extreme examples for this prologue. Week after week, for a number of years now, we have been faced with similar encounters. Time after time, we have witnessed the release of people in darkness into freedom in Jesus.

LEO

Satan is the master deceiver. Those who claim that he is a powerless relic from the unenlightened pages of antiquity have never met him face to face. He has as much power as Christians allow him to have.

Leo was highly respected in his cultural community as a man with awesome power. He presented an imposing figure with impeccable grooming and small, shining, emotionless eyes that bespoke the cold, frightening force within him.

Prominent people recognized his abilities to control intangible aspects of their lives and went to him regularly for power or vindication. If someone wanted to eliminate a troublesome person, for a fee Leo

13

would cast a spell and take care of the matter. If someone wanted another person to change in some way, Leo would simply perform a ritual and remedy the situation. If a man wanted his daughter to marry a particular person, he would pay Leo to ensure that the two would fall in love. On the other hand, if a young couple had marriage plans against the wishes of the parents, a trip to Leo and a healthy fee later, the two would suddenly break up.

Leo had over a hundred families under his control. Most of these were church going people who were deeply entrenched in the traditions of their particular denomination. However, when things began to go wrong for them, they would call on Leo who would think nothing of going out in the middle on the night in response to a call and work a spell over someone who was ill or in trouble of some sort.

Anyone not protected by the Lord Jesus was vulnerable to Leo's power to inflict physical or financial damage. The immediate source of his power was a powerful psychic in Italy of whom he was a disciple. A portion of the money collected by Leo for his services went to the psychic who continued to endue him with supernatural abilities from his master, Satan. The tools of Leo's evil ministry were a chalice, incense burners, candles and a church prayer missal. When he would place his hands on the missal, he would pray in the name of the psychic. Anyone permitted to watch his incantations would be awed by the otherworldly language he chanted during the rituals. No one ever dared cross him.

The amazing thing was that Leo saw himself as a benevolent community asset. Although he demanded payment for imparting spirits to people for their protection, at times he was a generous man, giving protector spirits to people who he liked and imparting them to babies as they were born into the community. His idol was Guilliano, the famous Italian bandit who robbed from the rich to give to the poor. He loved to think of himself as an all powerful, macho patriarch on whom people depended for all of their answers to life. The reality was that everyone feared Leo and stayed as far away as possible from him.

One of his married daughters, Maria, began to attend a Wednesday evening prayer group in our church. The Lord had been gradually introducing us to the realities of the spirit realm and we had shared some of the amazing things we had learned with the group.

As Carmen and I were entering the church one Wednesday, we were approached by a man who introduced himself as Maria's husband, Carlo. He was curious and yet very skeptical about some of the things Maria had shared with him.

"Do you believe in spirits?" he asked abruptly.

"Yes, of course I do", I replied. "There is one good Spirit and there are many bad spirits."

"No, no", Carlo shook his head impatiently. "I'm talking about the kind of spirits that stay with you all the time to help you out in life." He looked at both sides of his body.

Taking notice of the movement, I asked, "Are they with you now?".

"Yes", he replied. "They follow me wherever I go."

Since Carlo was obviously intending to see what went on in the meetings, we proceeded into the church and found a private place to continue our conversation.

"If these spirits are not of God, would you want them?", I asked.

"No", he replied, "but I don't want to hurt them. They're not doing me any harm. Why would I want to hurt them?".

"I'm not talking about hurting anything", I said. "I'm

15

just asking you if you want to get rid of them if they're not of God."

Carlo was a very religious man in the sense of being firmly entrenched in the traditions and superstitions of his denomination. However, he knew very little about the Word of God.

"Of course", he said. "I don't want them unless they are good for me, but how do I know if they are not of God?"

"Very simply", I replied. "Just tell them, in the Name of Jesus, that if they are not of God, you do not want them and they are to go."

After doing that, Carlo looked at the sides of his body and exclaimed, "What did you do with them? Where did they go?"

Obviously, the spirits had recognized the agreement in Carlo's heart with my instruction and had simply left.

Suddenly, Carlo became alarmed as he remembered that everyone in his family, including his wife and his children, had been endowed with spirits from Leo. If the spirits weren't of God, then they were harbouring evil spirits. He went home and with great concern recounted his experiences to Maria who, in turn, informed Leo of Carlo's release.

Leo was enraged that anyone should undo his work and attempted to reinstate the spirits. However, since Carlo had made himself right with God, Leo was unable to get any results from his incantations. He wanted to know who it was that had more power than he had.

The following week, Carlo brought his brother, Eduardo and their families to see us. They all wanted to know more about Jesus who had power beyond the father-in-law's powers. They all accepted Christ and, after a series of deliverances, were set free.

One evening when we were having dinner at Carlo

and Maria's home, Leo and his wife, Sophia, arrived. Leo stared at me with those flat, cold eyes of his and began to prod a bit for information about who we were. We made an appointment to meet with them at the church where we could speak at more length.

When they arrived, something held Leo back from entering and he could not get in the church door. There was nothing that anyone could do to get him to enter. Finally, we made another appointment with them but prior to the meeting, we bound the spirits from interfering.

This time, Leo and Sophia came in. Leo, chewing on a toothpick, sat down across from me. No more had I begun our meeting with prayer in the Name of Jesus, than Sophia got up from her chair and began wildly gesticulating and railing against me in a very strange language. She jabbed angrily toward the cross I was wearing, as though in furious rebuke.

Aware that I was not dealing with flesh and blood but spirits, I commanded Sophie to sit down, which she did for a moment. Suddenly she jumped up again saying, "They are hurting me! Make them stop!" as she tried to punch at me. Glaring at her husband, she jabbed with her finger at her chest and yelled, "*I want this house clean!*".

Confused, I wondered why she was talking about cleaning her house, until I realized that we were dealing far more in the spiritual realm than we knew. The "house" she referred to was her person.

As I began to explain to Leo the spiritual nature of Sophia's demands, I could see that he was not interested in the least in Jesus. All he cared about was the fact that I had more power than he did and he wanted to tap into my source. He questioned whether it had something to do with the cross I wore around my neck. It infuriated him to think that I could cast

17

spirits out of his children and nothing he could do would restore them! He asked us to visit their house the following week to tell him more.

At our next meeting, when I opened the Bible and began to show Scriptures to him concerning the love and power of Jesus, I encouraged Leo to look and read for himself. As he attempted to read, he became blind and couldn't see the page to read. When I attempted to read aloud to him, he became totally deaf.

Recognizing the enemy, I bound the powers of darkness and commanded them to release Leo's eyes and ears. As they let go, he suddenly got a throbbing headache and his whole head became freezing cold. In spite of my attempts to continue ministry and put the enemy in complete submission, Leo could stand the pain no longer and begged me to leave. They agreed to attend the prayer meeting at the church the following week.

Half way through the meeting, everyone was startled and turned in Sophia's direction as she began to yell at the top of her voice. Suddenly, she fell on the floor and began to turn and twist in writhing contortions. I bound the spirits in her, but to no avail. She continued her commotion.

I know now that God had us in His schoolroom that night. He prompted me to go to Leo and address the spirits in him that were ruling over his wife and family. God wanted us to understand the spiritual authorities and the workings of the dark kingdom.

Leo stared at me, surprised that I recognized him as the source of the problem. Sophia immediately quieted down, got up, brushed the floor dust from her dress and apologized in acute embarrassment.

By this time, it was painfully obvious to Leo that he was up against a power much greater than anything he had ever known. Sophia knew that freedom was an actual possibility through Jesus and she wanted release. We made an appointment for them to come to my office.

At first, Carmen and I focused on Sophia, but with little success. Again the Lord nudged us to turn our attention to Leo. No sooner had we begun to exercise our authority and pray over him than he began to act as though his chair was a horse and he began riding it! When I commanded the spirit to identify itself, it replied, "I am the Prince of Turkey and I am in charge here!". No matter what we did, it refused to budge. No release came. On a Holy Spirit hunch, remembering Leo's fascination with the Italian bandit, Guilliano, we tried binding the spirit of Guilliano. Immediately, Leo and the chair were thrown six feet across the room and with Leo screaming there was utter chaos. People in the building heard the commotion and came running. Leo pulled himself together to some extent, but he was panicky, realizing by now that his power was from the wrong source.

At our next meeting, before Leo and Sophia arrived, Carmen and I agreed to minister to them separately. Carmen had a prayer team in one room for Sophia and my team and I were prepared to minister to Leo in a room down the hall.

As the men and I commenced ministry with Leo, despite the distance between the rooms, Leo began to tell us everything that was happening in Sophia's room with Carmen and her team!

Again the Lord had us in His schoolroom. We realized that it was pointless to continue our efforts until Leo had more knowledge of the Word, repented and received Salvation.

Finally, after several more meetings, Leo received the Word and recognized the reality of the evil in which he had been involved. With a sincere desire to change, he repented and accepted Christ. However, despite his decision and regular attendance at our meetings, he still was not free.

On Leo's fifty-fourth birthday, he came to the church and declared his desire for release. He had an assurance that the Lord was going to set him free that night on his birthday.

Being aware of Leo's violent nature and very new to the deliverance ministry, I assembled a prayer team of eight strong men on the assumption that we would have to restrain him with physical strength.

Sure enough, as we began to bind the spirits, Leo began to get very violent and the eight men tried to control him but were having a great deal of trouble holding him back from attacking me. Had we known then what we know now, none of this would have been necessary.

All of a sudden, the Holy Spirit reminded me that demons must tremble and obey my words spoken in the Name of Jesus. I became filled with a faith and courage that I had never before known. With absolute authority, I commanded the demon to be bound and obedient and to get down on the floor. I told the men to let Leo go.

"No!", they protested, huffing and puffing through clenched teeth. "He will tear you apart if he gets at you!"

"Let him go", I repeated with rock solid faith. "The demons must bow before the children of God."

One by one, the men tentatively released their hold and Leo lurched forward as though to kill me. With absolute confidence I addressed the spirits: "I command you to bow down in the Name of Jesus".

Like a rock, Leo fell to the floor. Still trying to reach me, with his hands at his waist as though tied, he slithered toward me, tongue flicking in and out and shining red eyes actually bulging from their sockets.

Horrified, the men drew back in fear. Knowing the power of God within me, I commanded the spirit to come out of the man. Immediately, Leo went completely limp as though dead. I knelt beside him and prayed that God would fill him with His Holy Spirit.

As I assisted Leo to his feet, he knew that the ruling spirit was gone. His facial features actually changed before our eyes as complete peace replaced the sinister tension we had all come to know. He smiled the sweet smile of release that only those who know what it is to experience freedom from darkness can smile.

It took a few more meetings with Leo before he was completely free of all demonization. We showed him the importance of allowing the Lord to restore his soul through a process of repentance, forgiveness and allowing the Lord to heal his memories, but once he was free, he was a new man - completely changed.

Shortly thereafter, Sophia and the rest of their family came to know complete freedom in Christ as well.

The post script to this story has to be Leo's amazing gift of evangelism following his deliverance. He went to everyone whose lives he had controlled and told them his story of the love of Jesus. Many, many of those people received Salvation and were set free from the things that held them captive.

TERESA

In the early days of our ministry, we were invited to visit a pastor friend and his family in another province. We were looking forward to enjoying a wonderful holiday with them.

When we arrived, a call for help came from Teresa, one of their parishioners. The minister's wife had been counselling with Terri for some time, but had not felt that she was able to help her at all. The young woman had deep emotional problems and the minister's wife, knowing that we had some experience in the deliverance ministry, suggested that we should meet with her. She described Terri as "different, a very unusual person".

When we agreed to see her, our friend called Terri and arranged a meeting.

We went to her home and were taken down some dank steps to a basement apartment where we were introduced to an extremely introverted, depressed woman in her early thirties. She was hardly recognizable as a female with extremely short hair and drab, masculine attire.

When she saw me, she became very agitated and hostile at the presence of a man and absolutely refused to have a man present in her meeting with Carmen. That was fine with me and I offered to wait in the other room with our friend.

Carmen told me later that the first few moments with Terri were bizarre. Terri had sat with her arms folded angrily, her body language communicating absolute impenetrability. She stared first at Carmen and then at the empty chair and continued to alternate her focus. Carmen got an eerie feeling that they were not alone. "Is there someone else in this room with us?", she asked.

Terri nodded in the affirmative.

"Where?", Carmen asked.

Terri pointed to the chair.

"Are you afraid of it?", Carmen queried.

"Yes", replied Terri, "and it's really mad at me for telling you that it's here. It's glaring at me and grinding its teeth because it's so mad." She continued to tell Carmen a bit about the presence.

At that point, because we had not had much experience with deliverance and the Lord was in the early stages of teaching us, Carmen decided that she had better be afraid of the thing if Terri was. The one thing she felt capable of doing at that moment was calling, "Angelo!".

I ran quickly to the room where they were talking and found Carmen pointing to an empty chair in the corner of the room. "There's something else in the room with us. It's sitting on that chair."

I knew immediately what she meant. A supernatural being was present. She continued to explain. "The reason that Terri didn't want a male present is because this spirit is very jealous. It accompanies her wherever she goes and doesn't want any men around."

"Can you tell me a little bit more, Terri?", I asked.

"Well, it's about two feet high and it's all shaggy. It's with me wherever I go. If I go to church, it sits in front of me so that I can't see the minister. Usually I sit at the end of the pew because I'm afraid it'll hurt somebody. Sometimes when I'm driving, it sits on the steering wheel and I've almost smashed my car several times. If I don't do what it says, it'll beat me up. As a matter of fact, it's really mad at me right now for telling you about it."

"How does it communicate with you?", I asked.

"Telepathically", she said with a sigh of deep resignation.

"How long has it been with you?", I continued.

"Several years. It came to me while I was in the mental hospital and it has never left."

"What does it want?"

"It's my companion and my master. It has sex with me at night."

"But if it's only two feet high, how does it have intercourse with you?", I asked.

"At night, or whenever it wants to have sex, it turns

into a six foot tall monster. After it's satisfied, it grunts like a pig, rolls over and lies beside me on the bed."

"You mean it actually has an orgasm?"

"Listen", she said, "I used to be a prostitute. I've had enough men inside me to know what an orgasm is. Believe me, it does the whole thing. The worst part is, it makes me do things with other men and women and if I don't obey, it beats me up. One night, it told me that the woman from upstairs was coming down and that I'd better do what it told me to do to please her or it would beat me. That's when I became a lesbian."

"Have you tried to get any help before this?", I asked.

"Oh, yeah, sure. I started going to doctors because I was so depressed all of the time and they kept putting me in and out of mental hospitals. I've been to several psychiatrists and I've had a lot of group therapy."

"Did you tell any of the psychiatrists about the spirit?"

"Are you kidding? If I had, they would never have let me out of there."

"Where was the spirit while you were in group therapy?"

"It was there, sitting on a chair. Most of the time it just laughed because the doctors were unaware of the spiritual problem. They didn't know what they were doing. It knew that the doctors wouldn't get anywhere because it says I belong to it."

"Well we're just going to see who's in charge here", I said. In the Name of Jesus I bound the spirit and commanded it to leave.

"Oh", Terri said apprehensively. "It moved over to the corner of the room, but it's growling at me because you won't let it look back. It's warning me of what's going to happen tonight when I'm alone."

I realized that I hadn't been specific in commanding the spirit to leave for good. I had simply told it to leave and so it had vacated the chair for the corner of the room. At this point, I commanded it to depart completely from Terri and never to return to her."

"It's gone!", Terri exclaimed. "But will it come back and hurt me tonight?" After having lived in such dreadful circumstances for so long, she hardly dared hope for real freedom.

"It depends", I said. "If you know Jesus and refuse to let it return, then it cannot come back. However, if you don't truly know Him, then the spirit has a right to its own home and you can bet that it'll be back."

Although Terri professed to be a Christian, we knew that something was still holding her back. Carmen talked to her about spiritual warfare and how to remain protected. We prayed over her for protection and as it was getting late, we left assuring Terri of Jesus' ability to protect her and promising that we would call first thing in the morning.

Terri sounded excited when she answered our call. She said "I have something very important to tell you. It came to my door last night but it didn't come in. I did what you told me to do but it was so angry. It warned me that as soon as you go, it will come back and I'd better watch out then. I feel encouraged, but I'm afraid about what is going to happen. What should I do?"

We made an appointment to see her again for prayer and teaching on spiritual warfare. Despite the fact that the spirit was gone, Terri remained uncomfortable with my male presence. When I questioned her about why men made her uncomfortable, she couldn't answer.

As we continued to pray, the Lord gave me a word of knowledge. In my mind I saw a beautiful little brown horse tied to a tree near a fairground. A man of medium stature came and untied the mare. He picked up the little three year old girl who was with him and rode off toward a field. I described the horse, the man, the child and the location to Terri just as I saw them and asked her whether the scene had any meaning for her.

She began to shake and sobbed deep, wrenching sobs. She told us that I was describing in exact detail her step father and his horse and the day that he picked her up from the fair, took her to a field and raped her.

That was the beginning of years of torturous molestations and rapes of the little girl. The rest of her childhood was endured in submission to him until, as a young teenager, she finally ran away. It had been like jumping from the frying pan into the fire. Her home became a hippie commune where rape, perversion and occult dabbling was the norm.

Several abortions and too many men later, she ended up in a mental hospital where the spirit finally made its presence known to her.

Shaking her head in sadness, Terri recounted how she had never been able to sustain a relationship or a job. Until the recent kindness of an acquaintance had enabled her to secure her basement apartment, she had lived her entire adult life moving from one shack or trailer to another.

Through the same acquaintance she had come to the church looking for assistance with food and clothing. She got a bonus. She found Jesus.

It was overwhelming to Terri that the Lord actually cared enough about her to show me precisely what the root of her pain had been. That revelation allowed me to lead her to forgive her step father and to place her total trust in God. She knew that He would never have shown me all that He did unless He really cared about her.

Instead of carefree vacation days spent merrily with good friends, our holiday became a special time of teaching and caring for Terri. We remember it as a wonderfully rich time in learning more about the Lord and enjoying our sacrifice of service.

Terri called often and we built her up, encouraged her and strengthened her through Scripture. We warned her that we would soon be leaving and taught her to rest in the promises of Jesus.

As we shared more deeply with her, she relaxed and opened up and told us many horrible stories of her life under the control of this demon from Satan.

As the week progressed, we saw Terri transformed like a butterfly from a dark, restrictive cocoon. She expressed a desire to be called Teresa rather than Terri and when she arrived at church on Sunday, no one recognized her. For the first time in her life, she was dressed in pantyhose and a dress. No longer a defiant butch, she was a beautiful, feminine woman.

When Carmen commented on how lovely her dress looked, she glowed, "Really? You really like it?", with the pure delight of a happy child. It was an amazing transformation.

Some time after we returned home, we received a wonderful letter from Teresa. She was overjoyed that her step father had arrived unannounced and in deep contrition had requested her forgiveness. He gave her a considerable sum of money with which he hoped she would be able to make a fresh start with her life. What amazed her, was the fact that she had not contacted him and that he knew nothing about the fact that she had forgiven him. She was awed by the loving atmosphere of their visit, totally devoid of all fear or hatred.

Of course skeptics will say that the demon was a figment of the poor demented girl's imagination, perhaps drummed up and described to bring a measure of attention to an otherwise drab and lonely existence.

That conclusion might hold a measure of water were it not for the fact that in our experience alone, since our encounter with Teresa, we have come across many similar situations.

Over and over again, women have wept in shame as they have shared the horrors of their night visits. The pain and embarrassment of being sexually abused by a demonic power is almost beyond description. Sometimes the demons make themselves visible and in other instances they are experienced but not seen which is almost more horrifying. The effects are equally horrendous.

The phenomenon is really spiritual rape and has been recorded down through history as instances of spirits forcing themselves sexually on humans. Demons who have sex with women are recorded by the Greek term "Succubi" and those that demonize men as "Incubi". It would seem that sexual demonization is occasionally the result of inadequate expression of human sexuality and dissatisfaction with the situation which opens the door for demonic interference. At other times, as with Teresa, the probable entry point can be traced back to occult involvement such as contact with a Ouija board. Sometimes the spirits seem to arrive totally on their own, taking advantage of ignorance, weakness and lives lived apart from Christ.

Whatever the entry point, our experience in the deliverance ministry indicates that sexual demons enter as familiar spirits. From there they progress to molesting and raping their victims and finally control every aspect of their lives.

No matter how the skeptics may babble, those who

have experienced spiritual rape know what has happened to them. No amount of lofty philosophizing can erase the memories of haunted nights.

GLORIA

Gloria had heard of our ministry through Carmen's involvement in "Women Aglow". When she requested an appointment, Carmen suggested that she meet us at the church following another meeting that we had scheduled.

When she arrived, since I was late with the previous meeting, Carmen and her prayer team began the counselling session with Gloria.

Gloria's main concern seemed to be that she was unable to maintain a positive relationship with a man. She felt driven to have relationships, but after she had enticed a man into involvement with her, she would become irritable and unable to tolerate his presence. Having been married three times and discovering the same patterns emerging in this relationship that had destroyed the other two, she wanted help.

Gloria had accepted Christ and knew that leaving this relationship was not a viable option for her if she wanted to live a Godly life.

As Carmen began to pray for Gloria, I entered the room, having finished with my other meeting. As soon as I walked in, Gloria, who was facing Carmen with her back to me at the door, stretched her left arm out straight behind her, pointing at me and rebuking me in a loud, guttural voice.

"She does not like you", she said. "She wants nothing to do with you. You have no business here!"

Recognizing the voice as that of a spirit referring to Gloria in the third person, I told it to be quiet in the Name of Jesus.

As I sat down, Gloria jumped to her feet and began an

Indian war dance in accompaniment to her war whoops. She was wearing a bracelet that jangled and as she danced, the rhythm was identical to the sound of Indian drums.

When I commanded the spirit to identify itself, it pronounced a name which meant nothing to me, but sounded like an Indian god. I commanded it to tell me when it had entered Gloria and it proudly claimed that her father had offered Gloria to it when she was just a baby. Its name became his pet greeting for her.

"She belongs to me!" it boasted. "She is mine and no man can have her. I would kill her rather than surrender her to a man!"

With that, I simply declared Gloria's commitment to Jesus, commanded the spirit to be bound in obedience to Christ and told it to leave. She was free.

As Gloria regained her composure and was able to speak once again, she expressed shock at what had happened. She had had no idea that her father, who was of Indian descent, had dedicated her to an Indian god. She hadn't even realized that he had had much affiliation with the Indian culture. Her mother was English and their home had been typically white, Anglo-Saxon Protestant.

We met Gloria about a year later and, in response to our questions, she was delighted to tell us that she and her husband were doing very well. She appeared to be genuinely relaxed and happy.

Praise God.

CHAPTER ONE

MY PEOPLE PERISH FOR LACK OF KNOWLEDGE

Not long ago, a pastor stood behind the pulpit of a well known Evangelical Church and soothingly assured the congregation that as Christians they had nothing to fear from Satan. "Satan is nothing but a roaring lion", he preached. "His teeth were all pulled out at the Cross and now there's no way he can harm a blood bought child of God."

The Associate Pastor seated on the platform behind him nodded fervently in agreement and murmured, "Yes, amen. Amen".

The congregation listened and tried to relate their lives to his words. Joan's heart sank. Her husband, the Deacon at the back door, had been very repentant to her that morning after punching her in the stomach and threatening to break her arm the night before. His bouts of anger were becoming more and more violent. If Satan was not to blame for these attacks, what hope did she have since her husband was already a Christian?

Frank Cramer listened to the syrupy words with disdain. He wondered what on earth would come of the Christian Church if the Bible Colleges were turning out men trained in this dangerous theology. He had experienced deliverance from demonic oppression numerous times in his Christian walk and no one could tell him that he had not experienced what he knew had happened to him as a child of God. He knew that the men on the platform did not know what they were talking about.

THE DANGER OF IGNORANCE

Hosea 4:6 reads, *"My people perish for lack of knowledge"*. The second worst sickness in the world is ignorance. The absolute worst is not recognizing one's own ignorance.

When one is ignorant (meaning lacking knowledge or understanding) and knows it, he will try to protect himself by being careful about how he conducts himself. He will avoid making statements or decisions that could get him into trouble. The problem is that he will experience a lot of stress and tension as a result of his uncertainty in regard to his situation. He won't know what he can do and what he can't do - what abilities he has and what he doesn't have.

Recognized ignorance breeds fear - fear of making mistakes, fear of the past, fear of the future and fear of the unknown. Hospitals are full of people who know that they don't have a grasp on what is really happening in their lives and so they have turned their fears inward to eat away at their vital organs. Heart attacks, ulcers and disease are often the fruit of fear.

For a Christian, knowing that one is ignorant about what it really means to be a Christian in terms of rights and responsibilities, can be particularly disconcerting. Is he in or out of the will of God? Has he made the right or the wrong decision? How far should he go in ministering to others? He is always guessing, questioning, wondering, hoping that he has God's approval - but never resting in the confidence that comes from knowledge.

The good thing about knowing that one is ignorant is that it generates questions and motivates one to search for answers. As long as the searcher stays on track, ignorance will be replaced by knowledge and understanding. Genuine maturity will come.

On the other hand, not recognizing one's own ignorance is deadly. When people stand firmly on wrong
principles or beliefs, they live lives that lead them and
often others to disaster. Their dedication to their
convictions can and often do lead them to unnecessary and untimely deaths.

How about Jim Jones and his followers? Examination
of the lives of some of the people who died in that
garden of horror reveal moms and dads, sisters and
brothers not unlike some of our own. Many were
deeply spiritual people who sincerely wanted to live
for God. They simply made the mistake of blindly
believing a man instead of lining his words up to the
plumb line of God's Word. They didn't know that they
were ignorant.

The followers of David Koresh suffered some of the
most horrifying deaths imaginable because they didn't
know that the words their leader spoke were drawing
them away from the truth of God. They chose to accept
a man's perverted interpretation of Scripture over the
simple beauty of God's intent. There's nothing like
religion to capture and inebriate people, turning them
into puppets of designing charlatans. Almost without
exception, the life savings of sincere people are the
initial price they pay for being led into a nightmare of
deception.

BELIEF CAN BE DEADLY

Belief is the pivotal key to the choices we make. Belief
is the foundation of faith. Faith in Jesus is the very thing
that motivates a person to accept Him as Saviour.
However, if faith emanates from a wrong belief, it can
send a person to Hell just as surely as it can send him
to Heaven.

The problem is that faith is an intangible force based

on a metaphysical conclusion. In the spiritual realm, it is not something that can be put in a beaker and tested or verified in terms of any scientific deduction. There is no way of proving faith in a laboratory.

PUTTING TRUTH TO THE TEST
And so how do we know whether our belief system can be trusted enough to keep us from perishing as a result of lack of knowledge or destructive faith? There's one way.

God's intent, His instructions, His warnings and His plan are fully revealed in His Word. That is the plumb line by which all thoughts, philosophies and beliefs must be judged in order to know what is truth and what is not. Anything that deviates from the plumb line, even a little bit, is not worthy of using as a foundation for faith. If it deviates even a tiny bit in the beginning, the wedge will grow wider and wider as it continues, leading the seeker further and further from absolute truth.

The problem is that even if two people agree that the Bible is the final authority on all matters, they will no doubt interpret certain parts differently. Why? Experts tell us that we interpret what we read from our own perspective. We all have biases and unique approaches to life. We internalize things that are comfortable or convenient for us.

How then do we know which Scripture teachers are teaching truth and which ones are teaching according to their own agendas? How, indeed, do we know whether we ourselves are reading the Bible accurately or are colouring it according to our own comfort zones?

Jesus said that people with truth would be known by their fruit.

What does that mean? Well, fruit trees bear fruit,

unless they're completely barren. Some trees produce a great harvest while others are sparse in their production. Some fruit is absolutely delicious, totally ripe, full, juicy and gives abundant nourishment to anyone who is fortunate enough to eat it. Other fruit is not ripe, hard, bitter to the taste, small, unappetizing and lacking in nutrient value - perhaps even poisonous.

Galatians 5:22,23 says that, *"The fruit of the spirit is love, joy, peace, patience, kindness, goodness, faithfulness, gentleness and self-control"*. If other qualities than these predominate in the lives of those teaching us, there is a problem.

Jesus said, *"Watch out for false prophets. They come to you in sheep's clothing, but inwardly they are ferocious wolves. By their fruit you will recognize them. Do people pick grapes from thorn bushes, or figs from thistles? Likewise, every good tree bears good fruit, but a bad tree bears bad fruit. A good tree cannot bear bad fruit, and a bad tree cannot bear good fruit"* Matt. 7:15.

In order to be sure that we're getting truth, Jesus called us to be fruit inspectors. We need to look at the lives and ministries of those who claim to be teachers or ministers of the Gospel. Are they leading victorious, balanced, productive Christian lives, or are they always somehow behind the eight ball? What kind of victory are those under their ministry experiencing? Are they living the abundant lives Christ came to give them, or do they reflect the fact that they are missing some part of the Gospel in their lives?

Naturally, life is a process and everyone has challenges. However, if the pastor and his general congregation are living in more defeat than victory, the situation bears questioning.

DARING TO ACT ON GOD'S WORD - THE KEY TO SURVIVAL

In these days we need to be very daring. We need to dare to take God at His Word and believe everything that He says implicitly.

In order to keep from perishing, the knowledge we glean from God's Word has to be applied - in its entirety - to our lives. Having truth is only part of the picture. Application is the key to survival.

The great part about applying God's Word to our lives is that it's not a heavy duty task that we have to accomplish ourselves. God Himself loves us so much that He is just waiting to bless us and set us free from things that trouble us unnecessarily.

UNNECESSARY TRAGEDIES

How many people have perished because they have not known the depth of God's love for His children? How many have suffered lives of intense turmoil and pain, not knowing that if they had just reached out and asked God, He would have been there for them?

OUT OF THE MOUTHS OF BABES...

God is so egar to give..

I believe that God simply cannot resist the intense joy of supplying the need of a person who really trusts that He will respond to a cry for help.

When our daughter was a little girl we were barely nominal Christians and centred our Christmas festivities around the Santa hoopla. One Christmas Eve, about an hour before the stores were to close, she confided to my wife that she knew what Santa was going to bring for her. "In my letter to Santa," she whispered, "I asked him for a Wendy Walker Dolly. I promised him that I would be very, very good if he would bring it and I haven't been one bit bad, so I know that he's going to bring it tonight!" She put her chubby hands over her little mouth and giggled, her eyes shining in excited anticipation.

As Carmen looked at that precious little face, so trusting in its expectation, she realized that our little girl had been unusually diligent and happily coopera-tive. She knew that we had to be true to that trust.

She ran up to our room, frantically called me and told me not to leave my office until she had located a store with the doll. Praying and flipping through the Yellow Pages, she finally found a store that still had one, called me back with directions and I was able to secure it one minute before closing time. There was no price we would not have paid for that doll. We could hardly wait to see the delight on our little girl's face Christmas morning!

Would she have received that doll had she been taught that she would grow to be more mature without the doll, that the doll was just for others or that she had no right to take up anyone's time asking for it?

If we, as carnal humans, can have that level of love and desire to see our children blessed, how much more does our Father in Heaven want to see our smiling, happy faces lifted in thanksgiving to Him? When the desires of our heart are God's desires for us, faith is the key to unlocking the door to God's blessings.

WHAT ARE GOD'S DESIRES FOR US?

John 10:10 says, *"I have come that they might have life and have it more abundantly"*. Further on, in John 15:11, Jesus says, *"I have told you this so that my joy may be in you and your joy may be complete."* The second verse of the Third Book of John goes on, *"I pray that you may enjoy good health and that you will prosper, even as your soul prospers."* In John 15:7, Jesus promises, *"If you remain in Me and My words*

remain in you, ask whatever you wish and it will be given you. This is to my Father's glory, that you bear much fruit, showing yourselves to be My disciples."
People who preach a gospel of ill health, poverty and all kinds of pain are not only missing fullness in their own lives but are depriving their listeners of the wonderful life of freedom that Jesus came to bring. We don't advocate the "name it and claim it" brand of theology that has encouraged a grotesque, self-centred approach to Christianity, but we do believe whole heartedly in the promises of God.

Tragically, many people, Christian and non Christian alike, do not have any idea of the resources available to them through Christ, most specifically in the areas of spiritual warfare, healing and prosperity.

DELIVERANCE - A KEY ELEMENT IN JESUS' MINISTRY

Jesus spent approximately one third of His ministry teaching on spiritual warfare. Why is it seldom preached from the pulpits of our nations? Why do many pastors attempt to silence those who feel led to minister in that area? Why do they often dismiss as fanatics individuals who seek the deliverance Jesus promises? It is not my intention to criticize church leadership. I, myself, am a pastor.

I have, however, found in my ministry the amazing reality of the authority we have in the Name of Jesus to set people free from all kinds of things that many accept as simply the troubles of life. My desire is not to cause antagonism but to share with others the reality we have found in order to encourage them to step out with confidence into the blessings of God.

God knew that the churches would weaken and fail in their ministry as time passed. The Book of Revelation paints portraits of churches and their departure from the truth in the last days. He also spoke of those who hold fast to the truth enduring to the end. Let us be among those who walk in the power and authority of the Name of Jesus.

CHAPTER TWO

WHO ARE WE?

It is strange in these days of computerization, robots and mindboggling technology, how almost everyone in the world agrees that man is a highly spiritual being. The ancient Greeks didn't have a clue why they were on the planet. To them, existence was simply a mystery with no solution, an endless cycle going nowhere, accomplishing nothing. Jean Paul Sartre learned nothing from the intervening years of history but depressingly taught that we live as isolated freaks of chance in a purposeless world.

Almost universally, however, atheism and skepticism have been replaced by the 'new spirituality'. Humanists search within themselves to worship the 'god imminent' even though they continue to proclaim as 'fact' the Theory of Evolution which claims that we are simply cosmic accidents, unplanned results of cell multiplication. The New Agers flip through past lives and plan for the Declaration of Lord Maitreya.

Christians worship the risen Christ and see every human as a potential member of the Bride of Christ, the eternal companion of the Son of God.

OUT ON A LIMB

As the Twentieth Century draws to a close, more and more manifestations of the spirit realm have caught the attention of seeking hearts. Shirley MacLaine has fascinated audiences world wide on her trendy soapbox. Are we really, as she preaches, embodiments of roving souls living life after life after life? I have no doubt that she has experienced all sorts of spiritual adventures - where she really goes 'out on a limb' is in failing to recognize the demonic source of her experiences. They don't line up with the Word of God.

FILLING THE ACHING VOID

As the return of Christ draws closer, deep within the heart of every unredeemed person on the planet there is a deep stirring, an awakened awareness of the need within. God loves each one so deeply that He is wooing their hearts. The tragic part of it all is that in order to satisfy the uncomfortable spiritual void, many have rejected the Most High God of orthodox Christianity and have embraced a malevolent darkness that masquerades as light. They've become slaves of drugs, materialism, false religions, self - anything to try to fill the emptiness inside.

Who would want to turn to Christianity for answers when so-called Christian leaders down through the centuries have watered down the powerful message of the Gospel, for instance changing the powerful meaning of "meek and lowly" to 'weak and low', presenting Christians as wishy washy, dependent peasants who must resign themselves to enduring whatever storms buffet them as deserved disciplines from God?

It's time to wake up to the amazing truth of who Christians really are!

HONEST QUESTIONS - MUDDLED MINDS

Skeptical readers may ask, "How do you know that Eastern Mysticism, or the New Age Movement or the Moonies or whatever, are wrong and you're right? Where do you get off assuming that the Bible is true?

ELBOW GREASE

I do more than *assume* that the Bible is true. I *believe* that it is true as a result of extensive research and experience. Because this is not a book about proving the validity of the Bible, I leave the reader to do his or her own research. Christ paid a heavy price for our Salvation. Surely it is worth some time and study. Many people love to criticize Christian faith, but few are willing to get out the elbow grease, study and build a firm foundation for their ideas. Others may study but they read only the sources that they know are in agreement with their own particular biases.

WHO ARE WE?

The question remains, "Who are we?".

According to Scripture, we are a species of beings created for the purpose of eternal companionship with Jesus. However, because free will is such a foundational aspect of a meaningful relationship, that companionship happens only as a result of our desire to join our lives with His.

Once we choose to come into agreement with the purpose for our creation, the process of preparation to actually join Jesus on the Throne of the Universe begins. It is sometimes a very difficult process of education, training and maturing.

Redeemed humanity, those who have accepted the Spirit of God into their lives, are the highest order of beings in the universe. 1 Cor. 6:2 asks, *"Do you not know that the saints will judge the world?"*. The third verse goes on to ask, *"Do you not know that we will judge angels?"*. We outrank even angels! Angels are created beings, *"ministering spirits sent to serve those who will inherit Salvation"* (Heb. 1:14) We are not only created, but also generated. We are created in the full image of God.

When we are spiritually born (aka: born again, converted, new Christians), we become Children of God. Romans 8:17 is amazing. It says, *"Now if we are children, then we are heirs - heirs of God and co-heirs with Christ, if indeed we share in His sufferings in order that we may also share in His glory".*

Many people think that all of humanity are God's children. Not true. Until we choose to be spiritually adopted into the family of God, we are children of Satan (John 8:44).

THE QUALIFYING LEVEL

Earth is just the preliminary stage of eternity for us, the qualifying level. Some call it 'boot camp'. This is where we are expected to practice living as powerful spiritual beings. Before Jesus returned to the Father after His resurrection, He appeared to the disciples while they were eating and gave them the great commission (Mark 16:15): *"Go into all the world and preach the good news to all creation. Whoever believes and is baptized will be saved, but whoever does not believe will be condemned. And these signs will accompany those who believe: in My Name they will drive out demons; they will speak in new tongues; they will pick up snakes with their hands; and when they drink deadly poison, it will not hurt them at all; they will place their hands on sick people and they will get well."* As we dare to be obedient and trust that these things will happen, we see amazing supernatural power in our lives. The more we step out, the more we see happen and the more we become trained as mature believers.

THE BRIDE OF CHRIST

The group of people on Earth who believe that God planted the seed of His Son in a virgin, allowed the blood of Jesus to be shed in death as sacrifice for the sins of the world and then raised Him in a glorified body after three days to reign eternally, are called the

44

Church or the Body of Christ and will become His Bride at the Marriage Feast of the Lamb.

BARELY CATCHING A GLIMPSE

It is impossible to fully comprehend what the future holds for believers! 1 Cor. 13:12 says, *"For now we see as through a glass darkly, but then, face to face: now I know in part; but then shall I know, even as I am known."*

Our minds cannot handle more than a glimpse of what is ahead for us. 1 Cor. 2:9 goes on to say, *"No eye has seen, no ear has heard, no mind has conceived what God has prepared for those who love Him, but God has revealed it to us by His Spirit."*

FINALLY - UNITY!

Imagine. Believers will be in such absolute unity that we will function as one glorified mind. With all of the denominations and differences in theology that we have here on earth, that's hard to comprehend.

We think of our bodies as one organism because all of the parts of it are united and move according to the direction of one single consciousness or mind and yet Paul emphasizes the fact that our one body is composed of many different members, all having unique form and purpose.

In Ephesians 5:25, he speaks of Christ's plan for *"a radiant Church without stain or wrinkle or any other blemish, but holy and blameless."*

Some would say that there are going to have to be a lot of changes made before the dream of a spotless Church could be reality. However, let us not forget that the only purity we have is the covering of the blood of Jesus. We have no righteousness in ourselves.

The idea of presenting ourselves as pure and spotles

45

before Christ as products of our own efforts to be good is foolishness. There is no way it could happen. The natural heart of man is too wicked. In my mind, I picture each believer as standing before God, covered by a magnificent, red, velvety robe - the blood of Jesus - covering every sin and inadequacy.

In spite of differences in theology, personalities, cultures and ideas here on Earth, when people who really love God stand together in true praise and worship, a love for each other that transcends any differences is very much a part of their praise and worship. They sing as with one voice, one mind, one body of believers. I believe that that is just a tiny glimpse of the unity we will have in Heaven when we are able to love Christ face to face. A more beautiful relationship is impossible to comprehend.

THE FLY IN THE OINTMENT

However, there is a fly in the ointment.

When Jesus gave the great commission, the first sign that He said would accompany the believers was the driving out of demons.

Before the creation of the world as we know it, Lucifer was the mightiest angel in Heaven. Ezekiel 28:14-17 gives us a glimpse into his original stature and unceremonious fall. *"You were anointed as a guardian cherub, for so I ordained you. You were on the holy Mount of God; you walked among the fiery stones. You were blameless in your ways from the day you were created till wickedness was found in you. Through your widespread trade you were filled with violence and you sinned. So I drove you in disgrace from the Mount of God, and I expelled you, O guardian cherub, from among the fiery stones. Your heart became proud on account of your beauty, and you corrupted your wisdom because of your splendour. So I threw you to the earth…".*

Mighty, glorious Lucifer became Satan, God's enemy. One third of the angelic host rebelled against God and were thrown out of Heaven with Satan. With Adam and Eve's disobedience, sin entered the bloodline of man and the race fell out of union with God. This is commonly referred to as the fall of man.

Now Satan held legal title to the souls of mankind. The price for restoration of relationship with God was the shedding of innocent blood. Since sin was in the bloodline of all of mankind, innocent animals were sacrificed to remove the guilt of man before God.

However, since animals were imperfect creatures, it was only the shedding of Christ's innocent, perfect blood that paid the ransom for mankind once and for all time. There never has to be another drop of blood shed. It was finished at Calvary. Satan was defeated. All that remains is for believers to ask for forgiveness of their sin and appropriate what was done for them on that rugged cross in order to move from curse into blessing - from Satan's ownership into the Family of God.

NOW HERE'S THE RUB….

Although God defeated Satan completely through the cross, He allows him to carry on a sort of guerrilla warfare so that we can be trained in being over comers. If we are going to rule and reign with Jesus, then we have to know how. We have to learn to exercise our authority.

Knowing that we are much more than just temporal beings wandering around in cycles of despair and pleasure should give us a wonderful sense of hope in our high calling, respect for ourselves and rejection of anything that seeks to lower us to mar our positions as Children of God.

CHAPTER THREE

WE ARE IN AN INCREDIBLE BATTLE

"They're the Beautiful People of the '90's. They look as if they've strolled right out of the pages of GQ or *Harper's Bazaar*. Charismatic, clearly in command in any social situation, they exude the kind of killer confidence that says, 'I'm cool. I'm in charge. Nothing can touch me.' "

That is the opening paragraph of a feature article in the Toronto Star, Nov. 26, 1994. Who is the writer talking about? Models? Millionaires? Movie stars?

Vampires.

The article goes on to talk about the vampire fan clubs, books, movies and artifacts that are suddenly taking centre stage. "More and more, people apparently want to be like them. 'We have some members who believe they are vampires', says Eric Held, director of the Vampire Information Exchange in Brooklyn. 'There seems to be a rise of new books that portray the vampire as not necessarily evil, even as a good character who will fight for human beings. To get blood, (some of our members) practice self mutilation. They make cuts upon their own bodies or they get willing donors. They even ask them to take AIDS tests. They ask dentists to sharpen their teeth.' "

On Friday, Dec. 9/94, the theme of the Shirley Show on CFTO, Toronto, was vampires. Shirley appeared in a black cape and introduced eight people who were very serious about being addicted to drinking blood. They boldly discussed the various aspects of living as vampires as though no one should think twice about their lifestyles. Would they have been invited to participate in noon hour television even ten years ago?

The Los Angeles Times, March 12/93, reported a brisk business in an upscale area store called, *Necromance*. Among the 'chic' items for sale are human fingers on a leather cord, human skulls and necklaces of human teeth.

Common fare in any daily newspaper are items on Satanism, ritual abuse, incest, pedophilia, spousal murder, throwaway children, cannibalism, bestiality and every type of perversion imaginable. Just a few short years ago, homosexuality and lesbianism were beyond the pale, but now - they're old hat. They're an accepted part of the scene. Those who really want titillation now have turned to horrors so depraved that anyone with a clear mind has to weep.

John Walsh, host of *America's Most Wanted* told of a little two and a half year old girl who was kidnapped and kept in a van for three years while the kidnapper sold her to men for sex. Amazingly, she was rescued, but what was left?

Day after day the six o'clock news brings stories of new holocausts around the world. Images of tortured, emaciated bodies sear themselves into our minds. Didn't we say a long time ago that this would never happen again? Didn't we self-righteously judge the Germans for allowing atrocities to happen right under their noses? Why is it happening again, this time right out in full view on the world screen?

TAKING OFF THE BLINDERS

There is a battle going on and it has very little to do with guns and tanks. The opponents are God and Satan and the prize is human souls. The actual war was won when Jesus defeated Satan with His resurrection. However, just as battles and skirmishes continued for a short time after the Allies declared victory at the end of the Second World War, Satan is trying to take every piece of ground possible before his time is up. He knows that his time is short and he is trying to keep every soul he can from union with God. Keeping people in bondage to sin and ignorance concerning spiritual truths is his prime strategy. Those who have committed their lives and hearts to Christ are prime targets for destruction so as to draw them away from the heart of God.

Satan rages against Christians because he knows that we are God's elect and he is the defeated foe. He hates God and he knows that when we are afflicted with various difficulties, God feels our pain.

Ephesians 6:11-13 says, "*Put on the full armour of God so that you can take your stand against the devil's schemes. For our struggle is not against flesh and blood, but against the rulers, against the authorities, against the powers of this dark world and against the spiritual forces of evil in the heavenly realms. Therefore, put on the full armour of God, so that when the day of evil comes, you may be able to stand your ground, and after you have done everything, to stand*".

If this is not the day of evil, I hate to think of what that day will be like.

THE SOURCE OF OUR STRUGGLES

How much plainer can it be said? The real source of our struggles is not the tangible people or circumstances of our lives. We have a spiritual enemy who schemes against us causing all manner of dissensions in our relationships and troubles in our circumstances.

Does that mean that everything that goes wrong in our lives is Satan's fault - that there is a demon behind every miserable thing that happens to us?

No. We are exhorted in 1 Peter 1:13 to prepare our minds for action and to be *self-controlled*. Paul tells us in Romans 7:21-25 about the battle against the natural nature of man. "*I find this law at work: when I want to do good, evil is right there with me. For in my inner being I delight in God's law; but I see another law at work in the members of my body, waging war against the law of my mind and making me a prisoner of the law of sin at work within my members. What a wretched man I am. Who will rescue me from this body of death? Thanks be to God - through Jesus Christ our Lord. So then I myself in my mind am a slave to God's law, but in the sinful nature a slave to the law of sin..*"

Thus we are fighting our battles on four fronts - we fight to survive in this world; we fight our bodies which crave excessive gratification with food, sex, appearance, etc.; we fight against our own natures which are slaves to the law of sin and we fight directly against the schemes of Satan.

There are those who say that when people become Christians their old natures are purified and not subject to Satan's activities. So what does that say of Paul? Was he not a Christian?

If the truth were known, I believe that the extent of demonization is far greater than anyone imagines. In actual fact, I believe that there are very few believers who are not demonized in one way or another. No matter how mature a person may be in the Lord, the Christian walk is a process of releasing more and more of ourselves to Christ, of getting better and better at taking every thought captive. Satan never stops trying to draw us away from God.

As far as non-believers are concerned, Scripture tells us that they are all subject to demon powers. When the Lord appeared to Paul on the road to Damascus, He gave him a mission. Paul was to go to the Gentiles "*to open their eyes so that they may turn from darkness to light and from the dominion of Satan to God* (Acts 26:18). When he was addressing the Ephesians in regard to their spiritual condition before they became believers, Paul said, *"And you were dead in your trespasses and sins, in which you formerly walked according to the course of this world, according to the prince of the power of the air, of the spirit that is now working in the sons of disobedience* (Ephesians 2:1,2).

THE PIVOTAL FACTOR

When we accept Christ's sacrifice for our lives and ask forgiveness for our sin, our spirits come alive and we are washed clean of all guilt. However, our souls and bodies remain vulnerable to evil influence. The battle is fought in the mind and the pivotal point is the will. We choose whether or not to fall prey to Satan's temptations. If we do, we have to suffer the consequences of our choices.

BODY - SOUL - SPIRIT

While the redeemed spirit cannot be touched when it is filled with the Spirit of God, the soul and the body are not redeemed. The Christian walk is a process of renewing the mind, taking every thought captive and subjecting it to the Lordship of Jesus Christ, and being self-controlled with regard to the body, respecting it as the temple of the Holy Spirit within.

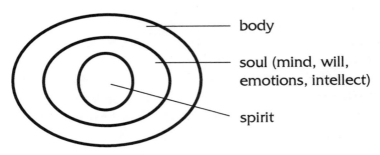

body

soul (mind, will, emotions, intellect)

spirit

CHECKING OUR BAGGAGE

When we initially accept Christ, we come to Him carrying years of baggage and bad habits. For the most part, those do not magically disappear at the moment of conversion. They remain with us until, one by one, we submit each area of our lives and each unprofitable habit to the Lordship of Jesus. We allow Him to change us step by step. However, that submission is generally not just a passive act of handing over. There is often a great deal of wrestling whatever it is away from Satan's control before it can really be handed to Christ.

OPENING THE DOOR TO THE ENEMY

The problem is that when we give in to temptation or even when we harbour ungodly thoughts, we open a door that gives Satan opportunity to act in our lives. For instance, if a married woman were to become attracted to an office coworker, she has the choice of acting on her thoughts and becoming romantically involved with the person - or totally rejecting the thoughts every time they enter her head - or (and this is often where grave problems arise) simply entertaining the thoughts, enjoying the pleasurable feelings they produce in the belief that as long as she doesn't take any action, she's O.K. What she doesn't realize is that if she entertains lustful thoughts, she can unknowingly invite a spirit of lust to take up residence in her soul. At this point, the control she once had over the thoughts becomes uncontrollable and the only way to be free of the thoughts is by being delivered through spiritual warfare.

While our focus in this book is on the dark forces with which we have to battle and how to be free of them, it is very important to recognize that they are not the only source of our struggles. However, it is equally important to recognize that they are one major source. It has become distasteful in many churches to even suggest any discussion of demonic activity, in spite of the fact that one third of Jesus' ministry dealt with how to overcome evil. Anyone knows that the first rule in any battle is to know your enemy. The second is to face him and the third is to rout him. Trying to ignore an enemy who is bent on your destruction is utter foolishness. Yet that is exactly what is happening - and why Satan *appears* to be winning this one.

KNOW YOUR ENEMY

Most people believe in an evil power of one sort or another. However, because the spiritual realm is usually invisible, they don't know much about it and try to avoid any contact with it. They think it is 'spooky' or 'weird'. Even many Christians take the 'hands off' approach because they don't really know who they are in Christ and they fear Satan and possible reprisals if they do anything that might make him notice them. Little do they understand how Satan and his troops tremble when faced with a confident Christian.

As much as Satan wants to keep people in ignorance, Scripture provides us with a clear bio on our enemy. The name *Satan* comes from Aramaic origin. It means adversary (one who opposes another in purpose to act). He is the inveterate adversary of God and Christ. He incites apostasy from God and to sin. The worshippers of idols are said to be under his control. (Matthew 4:10, Zechariah 3:1) There are numerous terms in Scripture which refer to Satan:

* *Devil* - From the Greek word Diabolos meaning false accuser, the slanderer, Satan, the prince of demons. Persecuting good men, estranging mankind from God and enticing them to sin, afflicting them with diseases by means of

demons who take control of their bodies at his bidding. (Matthew 4:1, John 8:44)

* *Lucifer* - (bearer of light) name given to Satan before the fall. (Isaiah14:12) Ezekiel 28:13 and Isaiah 14:11indicate that he was a master musician.
* *The Anointed Cherub who Covers* - (Ezekiel 28:14) Before the fall Satan was responsible for guarding the throne of God.
* *Serpent* - A snake. (Genesis 3:1, Revelation 12:9)
* *Trapper* - (Psalm 91:3)
* *Beelzebub* - (Matthew 12:24,27) "Lord of the flies" - a dung god of the Ekronites.
* *Enemy* - (Matthew 13:39)
* *Ruler of the Demons* - (Matthew 12:24)
* *Tempter* - (Matthew 4:3)
* *Evil One* - (Matthew 13:19)
* *Murderer* - (John 8:44) Destroyer of life.
* *Liar* - (John 8:44)
* *Ruler of the World* - (John 12:31, 14:30, 16:10) When Satan tempted Jesus, he spoke as though all of the kingdoms of the world were his. Jesus did not dispute him.
* *Wolf* - (John 10:12)
* *Thief* - (John 10:10)
* *Antichrist* - (I John 4:1-4, 2 John 7)
* *Oppressor* - One who has dominion over. (Acts 10:38)
* *Angel of Light* - (2 Corinthians 11:14)
* *Deceiver* - (Revelation 12:9, 2 Corinthians 11:3)
* *God of this World* - (2 Corinthians 4:4)
* *Prince of the Power of the Air* - (Ephesians 2:2)
* *Belial* - Worthless, perverse. (2 Corinthians 6:15

* *Adversary* - (I Peter 5:8)
* *Roaring Lion* - (I Peter 5:8)
* *Dragon* - (Revelation 12:3-17)
* *Condemner* - (I Timothy 3:6)
* *Angel of the Abyss* - (Revelation 9:11)
* *King* - Revelation - (Revelation 9:11)
* *Abaddon or Apollyon* - Destroyer. (Revelation 9:11)
* *Accuser* - (Revelation 12:10)

Ezekiel 28:13-15 establishes that he was created by God. Isaiah 14 and Ezekiel 28 tell about the high position he held in Heaven before pride got the better of him and his self-will got him cast out of Heaven with a third of the angelic population who followed him (Revelation 12:4-9).

According to Jude 6, some of these fallen angels are freely going about their malevolent work here on earth, awaiting confinement, while others who dared leave their appointed realm are already held in eternal bonds under darkness awaiting Judgment.

A GUIDED TOUR

A close friend of ours, whose wife was praying fervently for his salvation, was taken to Heaven and Hell in a vision and was shown the consequences of not accepting Christ. He was taken before Satan and he recounted later that had he not been under the protection of Jesus, he would never have survived the encounter. He described Satan as a huge, magnificent creature who was the absolute embodiment of evil. Although he never actually saw his face, he was overwhelmed by the awesome blackness of raw horror.

THE DARK KINGDOM

Because Satan is neither omnipresent nor omnipotent,

he has to rely on his organizational skills and his demon spirit troops to maintain his position as ruler of this world. Ephesians 6:12 gives us some insight into the highly organized confederacy of evil spirits. It speaks of four separate designations:

- principalities
- powers
- rulers of this darkness
- spiritual forces of wickedness in the heavenly places.

The *principalities* refer to territorial spirits. Satan has assigned each territorial spirit a specific geographic location to rule and complete a particular mission of darkness. For instance the story of the prince of Persia in Daniel gives us a glimpse of how specific spirits operating above a country (Persia in this case) work through the government of that area. People in each area become accustomed to the particular ruling spirit and, unless they are sealed by the Holy Spirit, they are like puppets dancing to the tune of an unseen piper. If we could see into the spirit realm, we would be amazed at how much we can effect our areas and nations through our prayers.

The *powers* refer to demon spirits that seek fulfilment of their particular natures through human bodies. Their mission or function is to afflict and torment humans with the goal of keeping them away from the love and blessings of God. Their characteristics are more fully discussed in Chapter Seven.

The *rulers of this darkness* are experts in their field. They specialize in certain areas of torment and they control the powers which demonize humans. For instance, unclean spirits rule spirits of pornography, bestiality, homosexuality, incest and anything that seeks to defile the body.

Spiritual forces of wickedness in heavenly places refer

to Satan's lingering battle with the High Courts of Heaven. Satan goes before God daily accusing the saints, saying things like, "You expelled me from Heaven because of my pride. Look at Jennifer. What about her? She's full of pride and yet she calls herself a Christian. If You're a just God, You need to expel her from Your Kingdom."

THE KINGDOM OF LIGHT

However! Jesus is our advocate before the Father. In spite of any truth in Satan's tales to the Father, if we repent we have no worries because Jesus reminds the Father that our sin has been covered by His blood. The fruit of repentance is a change in our attitudes and that is all God asks. It closes the mouth of the adversary. The prodigal was in right standing with his father as soon as he had a change of heart. His father did not wait for him to be dressed in fine linen before enfolding him.

SATAN'S LIMITS

Although Satan is very powerful and wields great influence over our lives, his power is limited to what God allows him to do in our lives.

Perhaps the clearest example of this is the story of Job. Initially, Satan was unable to touch Job. However, upon debate, God lifted a measure of His protection over Job and his family and possessions in order to demonstrate Job's faithfulness to God. Step by step, Satan was able to operate only within the realm of his permission from God.

Again in the New Testament, Luke 22:31-32 records Jesus, in his response to the disciples' question about who was greatest, telling Peter that Satan wanted to put him through some hard things, but that He (Jesus) had prayed for him. *"Simon, Simon, behold, Satan has* demanded permission to sift you like wheat; but I have prayed for you, that your faith may not fail." Satan was given permission to put Peter to the test, but he could only do what the Lord allowed, and Jesus was right there praying that Peter's faith would not fail. Following Peter's devastating experience with the crowing of the cock and his denial of Jesus, Jesus restored Peter body, soul and spirit.

Satan is limited not only in power, but also in time and location. Revelation 12:12 tells us that Satan has only a short time before he will be bound. Obviously, the demon spirits are well aware of this because in Matthew 8:29 when Jesus was casting evil spirits out of a man, they protested loudly, crying, *"What do we have to do with You, Son of God? Have You come here to torment us before the time?*

Job 1:6-7 clarifies the fact that Satan is not omnipresent. He can be in only one location at a time. Only God is omnipresent.

Perhaps Satan's greatest weakness is his lust for worship. He wants to be the revered, almighty one to whom every being bows.

THE DESTINY OF OUR ENEMY IS SEALED

However, his destiny is sealed. Satan and his evil troops have no hope of glory. Revelation 20:10 tells us that, *"the devil who deceived them was thrown into the lake of fire and brimstone, where the beast and the false prophet are also; and they will be tormented day and night forever and ever"*.

The tragic thing is that everyone who fails to enter into life with Jesus will share this awful destiny. God did not create Hell for humans. He created it for Satan and his followers. It is up to each individual whether to follow Jesus to Heaven or Satan to Hell. Eternity awaits.

THE WEAPONS OF OUR WARFARE

2 Corinthians 10:4,5 says, *"The weapons we fight with are not the weapons of the world. On the contrary, they have divine power to demolish strongholds. We demolish arguments and every pretension that sets itself up against the knowledge of God, and we take captive every thought to make it obedient to Christ"*.

That phrase '*take captive*' makes me think of a cowboy charging after a calf, swinging his lariat and lassoing it - taking it captive and bringing it into submission to him, a very aggressive, purposeful action. It speaks of a confident, offensive manoeuvre designed for victory, giving no place to compromise, sometimes swinging again and again until the calf is secure or the thought is taken captive.

The problem is, that for every cowboy in the ring bringing a calf into submission, there are thousands of flabby onlookers in the stands. That's too often the way it is in Christianity. For every believer wrestling against spiritual powers and taking every thought captive, there are thousands of lazy Christians not walking in victory because they simply allow the enemy free rein in their lives.

What are the weapons we have been given that have divine power to demolish strongholds? They are the Blood of Jesus, the Name of Jesus, the Word of God, praise, praying in tongues, fasting, anointed music, the gift of discerning of spirits and the word of our testimony.

RECOGNIZING THE REALITY OF THE BATTLE

Before becoming Christians, most people are unaware of the reality of the battle that surrounds us. They simply live in a world of apparent ups and downs without questioning roots and sources of situations and relationships.

One young couple came to us some time ago in great confusion. They had been in the entertainment business making four thousand dollars a week before they became Christians. Because they became uncomfortable with their type of entertainment after meeting Christ, they abandoned their careers. However, because they had no other skills, the only work available to them was manual labour. They went from an excellent income to five hundred dollars per week. Their lifestyles changed dramatically. Their friends and relatives would have nothing to do with them and sneered at their new beliefs behind their backs.

It didn't take long for the young couple to recognize opposition once they stopped walking Satan's line. It was very difficult for them to feel totally ostracized by the very people who had claimed devotion to them such a short time before. However, they hung on to their faith and the joy they found in knowing Christ carried them through their initial difficulties. They found that the struggles they endured deepened their commitment and caused them to grow into a strong Christian family.

DECEPTIVE RECRUITMENT

Over and over again I've had new Christians come into my office complaining that everything was fine until they became Christians. Then, they say, they got sick, lost their jobs, had accidents or whatever. I always ask the same question: "Were you told that this might happen when you accepted the Lord Jesus?". Invariably the answer is "no".

If I have one problem with Christian evangelists, it is that many of them seem to think that they have to con people into the Kingdom. They imply that all they have to do is accept Jesus into their hearts and bingo! Their lives will be nothing but love, joy and peace.

What ever happened to the magnificent revelation of Christ's death in our place and His resurrection that rescues us from the clutches of eternal damnation and promises eternal life in Glory to those who love Him? Where is the gratitude for His inestimable sacrifice? What is more important in the salvation they offer - relationship with the Jesus who gave His all for us, or a cushy life of love, joy and peace?

It's true that accepting Christ is the most wonderful step we ever take in life. However, it's often also the beginning of struggles - struggles with Satan, with old habits that die hard and with the demands of our flesh which scream for satisfaction. Our eyes must be firmly fixed on the rewards of Eternity rather than earthly comfort.

STRENGTHENING THE TROOPS

As humans, we long for approval from our friends and families. When new Christians, who may have lost their old support base as a result of their conversion, begin their faith walk, they may experience tremendous isolation. The transformation period may be very painful for them until they really learn to hear from God who will sustain them.

When people come to Christ, it is of paramount importance that the Christian family surround them, nurture them, teach them and help them to unwrap their grave clothes, those things that have kept them bound and unable to enjoy freedom in Christ.

REALITIES

Make no mistake. When we come to Christ, Satan is not happy. Remember his pride? It was so great that he had the audacity to challenge God for preeminence. When a simple human gathers the intestinal fortitude to reject Satan in favour of God, Satan gets backhanded with rejection and he makes things as difficult as he can for the new Christian. Fortunately, it's never more than we can bear because we are covered with the protection of Almighty God.

Where he once controlled us, now we are given the tools to control him. Where he once had power over us, we now have power over him. Where he was once a danger to us, we are now a danger to him. He has good reason to slow our growth as much as possible in order to minimize the danger to him.

If he can, he will kill us to prevent us from spreading the good news. Make no mistake. Our guardian angels lead busy lives.

Failing elimination, he may attempt to discredit us through planting unwise plans in our minds etc. He may attempt to get us to blame God for the problems he throws in our paths. He may inflict us with illness, poverty or whatever and then tauntingly point his finger at God and sneer, "If God is so great, why do you have all of these problems?".

WE WRESTLE - WE WRESTLE NOT

And so we wrestle to survive. We wrestle not only with the world in which we live, but with our own natures and with Satan himself. He wants control of our minds and bodies. We are in an all out battle with the enemy of our souls. However, knowing the authority we have been given over him gives us the confidence to face adversities without fear.

The greatest problems come when we wrestle not. One of Satan's most common tactics is to get us so exhausted and discouraged from our battles that we simply give up and stop fighting.

The good news is that we are not powerless, but have the resources of the entire Heavenly host at hand. We have work to do. Help is just a whisper away.

In Matthew 10:22, Jesus promised that, "*he who stands firm to the end shall be saved*".

We must remember that this is just a battle. No matter how tough things may get, it's just a battle. The war has been won and we're on the victory side.

CHAPTER FOUR

THE POWER OF A CHRISTIAN

I'll never forget the story of a young girl, proudly living on her own for the first time in her own apartment who learned the reality of her power as a Christian in an extraordinary way. One day, late in the afternoon, she had just returned from work. A knock came at her door and as she opened it a crack to see who was there, a rapist violently shoved the door open and forced his way in. He commanded her silence and, ferociously brandishing a knife, threatened that if she made one sound he would kill her. Like a trapped rabbit, her eyes fastened in horror on the raw evil in the eyes of her assailant.

She thought that her heart would pound right out of her chest.

Into her mind popped the words, *"No weapon formed against you shall prosper"* Isaiah 54:17. She remembered her dad at home telling her that if she ever came up against anything that she knew to be evil which threatened her safety, she had the authority as a Christian to rout it. Ever since she had been a tiny girl, her family had gathered every morning after breakfast for a reading of Scripture. It had been ingrained in her that Satan could not prevail against the Word of God. The knowledge of her position as a Christian welled up inside her and with a strength not her own, she stared into the eyes of the intruder and declared through trembling lips, "You can't touch me with that knife because Scripture says that no weapon formed against me shall prosper".

Fear suddenly registered on the man's face and he turned and ran out of the apartment. He went to another door where a woman answered his knock and he raped her instead. Of course the first girl called the authorities and the man was caught as he attempted to leave the building. In his trial, the man was asked why he had left the first apartment without harming the young girl. He answered by asking, "You think I'm gonna stay there with those two huge guys who showed up in her apartment?". She had been alone - she thought.

Hebrews 1:14 asks, *"Are not all angels ministering spirits sent to serve those who will inherit salvation?"*. That young woman will never forget the power available to her as a Christian.

THE AUTHENTICITY OF MARK 16:17

Mark 16:17 is a remarkable scripture. In it, Jesus says that, *"These signs will accompany those who believe: in My Name they will drive out demons; they will speak in new tongues ..."*. Skeptics have tried to deny its authenticity by claiming that the most reliable early manuscripts do not contain verses nine through twenty of that chapter. Many people throughout recent centuries have been trapped into doubt about healing and deliverance through their contention.

According to the Russian scientist, Dr. Ivan Panin, who established Bible Numerics (not Numerology!) and wrote *Amazing New Discoveries*, the passage in question has all of the remarkable features particular only to canonized scripture. It therefore has to be authentic Scripture.

In fact, there are 4,200 Greek manuscripts of the New Testament. Of these, at least 680 contain the Gospel of Mark and only two are missing the passage in question. There are 8,000 Latin versions in existence and all of these contain Mark 16:9-20.

Of the two manuscripts that do not contain the passage, one has a blank space at that point, presumably for the passage, while the other is missing not only the passage in question, but also Genesis 1-46, Psalms 105-137, Hebrews 9:14 and 13:25, all of ITimothy and IITimothy, Titus, Philemon and Revelation.

I therefore make no apologies about resting heavily on Jesus' promise in Mark 16:17. Let's look at it again. *"These signs will accompany those who believe: in My Name they will drive out demons; they will speak in new tongues ..."*. What an incredible thing! According to this, anyone who really believes should have supernatural signs evident in his or her life. Believers should be sending demons packing as a matter of course. It shouldn't be any strange deal. It should simply be part of the Christian life for any believer.

REAL CHRISTIANITY

Luke 10:17-20 says, *"The seventy-two returned with joy and said, 'Lord, even the demons submit to us in Your Name'. He replied, 'I saw Satan fall like lightening from Heaven. I have given you authority to trample on snakes and scorpions and to overcome all the power of the enemy; nothing will harm you. However, do not rejoice that the spirits submit to you, but rejoice that your names are written in Heaven' "*. If Jesus gave believers the authority to rout demons, why are we not seeing evidence of that in the church today?

There are those who say that the supernatural manifestations of the power of God in believers was given only for the establishment of the church on earth and are no longer necessary. If that is true then why did God give the gift of discernment of spirits to the church? Did He not expect the believers to do something about them?

JOLTED INTO REALITY

In 1975, Carmen and I were brand new Christians. We were in the Catholic Church at the time and we were asked to help out with an Italian charismatic group. They needed a leader and because my English was better than that of most in the group, I was put in charge.

Training for leadership consisted of an hour or two one evening and I was instructed to pray over the sick and needy people. It was truly a case of the blind leading the blind.

My knowledge of Scripture was sketchy at best. The only positive thing that can be said is that I believed every word that I knew. My wife and a priest were to assist me. What I did not know then was that God had a plan for us and, as the true leader of the group, He was about to make some very unusual moves.

The first night, a member of the group brought a lady to the meeting who was in terrible pain. We were told that at times it was so bad that she would lose total control of herself. During particularly severe bouts her family felt that they had no alternative but to lock her in a room where she would sometimes stay for days; kicking, screaming and rolling on the floor like a wounded animal. Doctors had performed many exploratory surgeries to find the source of the pain but could find nothing.

She looked terrible. Her countenance was the most tormented that I have ever seen. Her skin was leathery and wrinkled from all of the painful contortions the pain had forced upon her face. She had no teeth because they had been removed to keep her from biting her tongue. Her clothes were ragged from lack of care and she walked as though she was ninety years old.

When I invited her to sit down, I sensed some

resistance and was very surprised when she began to engage me in a conversation about scripture and spiritual matters. It didn't make any sense to me because most Italian women of her age at that time were illiterate. Few had any schooling and she certainly did not have the bearing of an educated woman. Besides that, the Bible simply was not read by ordinary Catholic people in those days. It was left to priests to interpret scripture to the people of their parishes. How did she know so much about the Bible and the spirit world?

It did not occur to me that the spirits within her knew Scripture backwards and forwards.

As such a new Christian myself, I felt very inadequate to enter into any kind of debate and besides that, I was uncomfortable talking with her. In an attempt to take control of the situation, I indicated a chair where I wanted her to sit down and told her that we were going to pray for her.

Quite frankly, I had no idea what to do and so I began to pray in tongues, trusting that the Holy Spirit would show me how to proceed. No sooner than I had begun than she let out a scream like a mortally wounded beast. Every head in the church turned to see what had happened. I was told later that even some people outside had heard that scream and wondered what on earth was happening.

As the woman shrieked, her legs and arms stretched straight out towards me. She struggled to move but seemed locked in that position.

My wife looked at me, her eyes silently beseeching, "What do we do now?". Beads of perspiration popped out on the priest's forehead and in nervous agitation he exclaimed, "I hope you know what you are doing!". I returned my wife's frozen stare. I had never witnessed anything in my life like this before.

In a flash of pure inspiration, I commanded the woman to 'be quiet!'. I was probably more surprised than anyone when she was suddenly relaxed and still. Knowing that I was beyond my depth, I suggested that we postpone prayer until I had some more experienced help.

A few days later, for the first time in my life, I witnessed a deliverance. By the grace of God, the woman was totally set free in the Name of Jesus. Every vestige of pain left her body. Her once twisted countenance became smooth and miraculously peaceful as sweet tears of release coursed gently down her pain worn cheeks. It was a sight that I will never forget.

That experience caused me to do a lot of thinking and praying. I knew that if I was to continue to lead the group, I needed to grow quickly in the Holy Spirit. I asked him to teach me.

THE DREAM

That week I had a dream. It was so clear that to this very day, almost twenty years later, I can recall almost every detail. I dreamed that I was in someone's back yard where a small pond had been dug and filled with crystal clear water. A canvas covered half of it.

As I stood chatting with some others by the water's edge, a small child wandered by. No one seemed to be looking after her and I became apprehensive as she seemed drawn to the water. Suddenly, she fell in and began to drown. No one made any move to help.

Without hesitation, I jumped in to save her. As I grabbed the little body, I saw three huge snakes in the water at the other side of the pond begin to swim swiftly towards us. I tossed the child out of the water on to the grass and jumped out myself as fast as I could. I seized the edge of the canvas and pulled it over the entirety of the pond in an effort to contain the snakes and keep them from coming out of the water. There was a baseball bat lying nearby and I grabbed it. By this time, I could see the shape of the heads of the snakes pushing against the canvas, trying to get to us. With all of my might, I smashed the bat against the canvas where the heads were, over and over again until the snakes were no longer a threat. The canvas was stained red with their blood.

I looked around at the people, shocked at their indifference. They had shown no concern for the drowning girl and now that she had been rescued, it was obvious that they weren't even going to acknowledge that there had been a problem, much less a life saved.

I cried, "Lord, what do You want me to do?". I felt a strong sense of responsibility and Fatherly approval. As I wakened, I shuddered at the dream and wondered what it meant.

The next day, I got a call from a lady who had heard about the woman who had been set free from pain. She, too, needed help. I invited her to come over and as Carmen and I prayed for her, she expressed three distinct sensations of heavy burdens being lifted from her person. Then I thought of the dream - three snakes, three releases, three spirits cast out. As we continued to pray, she was set free in much the same way that we had seen the other woman released.

GROWING IN WISDOM, KNOWLEDGE AND STRENGTH

Encouraged by the difference we saw in the lives of the women, we continued to pray for people to be set free from all kinds of things that were troubling them. We sought the Lord fervently to teach us to be sensitive and responsive to His voice. We studied

Scripture and bought every book available on the subject of deliverance in an effort to become as knowledgeable as possible. Some made sense and others did not.

We began to see a lot of results from our praying and consequently became bolder and bolder in confronting the realm of the spirits. I began to get quite proud of myself.

One night as I slept, I was suddenly awakened in a cold sweat, tormented by an intensity of fear that I have never felt before or since. Even during the war, as I lay in the trenches with bombs dropping all around me, I never knew the fear that I experienced that night. I dared not open my eyes because I knew that Satan was in the room. Curled in a frozen knot in the fetal position, I knew that I had to address Satan.

Barely audibly, I declared that I was not afraid of him and that the longer he kept me awake, the longer I would praise the Lord Jesus. No sooner had I said that than the fear totally left and I experienced the sweet, sweet peace of the presence of Jesus. I knew that the Holy Spirit was there to protect me as long as I would stay close to Him and call on the Name of Jesus.

Comforted by that experience, I had the Christ-confidence necessary to lead the group and I took charge of the ministry willingly and with fresh determination.

Since that time, we have continued to grow and move in the Holy Spirit in ministering to people. We now expect the supernatural as a natural part of prayer ministry to people. We know that as Christians we have amazing resources of power. All we have to do is put ourselves in line with Scripture, rest and believe in the supernatural power of God to work through us as available vessels. We never know what He is going to do. It is, after all, His work.

HAVING A FORM OF GODLINESS

It must be so frustrating to God to have made such amazing provision for us and then to see us flounder around in all sorts of unnecessary difficulties simply because we allow Satan to buffet us. There is so much more to Christianity than most people experience.

2Timothy 3:1-5 paints a vivid portrait of our world. *"There will be terrible times in the last days. People will be lovers of themselves, lovers of money, boastful, proud, abusive, disobedient to their parents, ungrateful, unholy, without love, unforgiving, slanderous, without self-control, brutal, not lovers of the good, treacherous, rash, conceited, lovers of pleasure rather than lovers of God -* **having a form of godliness but denying its power.** *Have nothing to do with them."*

We must be so vigilant in these days not to be part of the shiny 'Christian lifestyle' where acceptability seems to rest on squeaky clean appearances and where Spiritual devotion is shunned as 'fanatical'.

I was speaking the other night at a meeting. I shared deeply from my heart and very openly about some experiences where the Lord had taught us and nurtured our growth.

A beautiful young mother approached me afterwards and implored me to talk with her. She couldn't believe how straightforwardly I had spoken. She said, "You know the people in this church are really great and they've been so kind to us, but if they had any idea of what I am going through, they wouldn't believe it. Sometimes I wonder whether they are even real. They all act so nice and they don't seem to have any problems. When I'm here, I pretend that everything is normal in my life because I don't want them to think that I'm weird or anything but I'm going crazy. I feel as though if I tell anybody about how I really feel, they'll look at me as if I'm from another planet. Actually, I only come to this church for special events because there doesn't seem to be much point in coming except to bring my kids for the children's program."

Of course we talked and I made an appointment to talk further with her the following day, but her dilemma was heartbreaking. She had taken her struggles to the one place she should have been able to find release but didn't dare share them for fear of being ostracized. It was like a severely wounded person going to a hospital for help but struggling to keep her bandages on so that the doctors and nurses wouldn't see any blood and turn up their noses.

Churches need to be like hospitals - places where sick and troubled people can find hope and healing - and places where strong, spiritually healthy people focus on being vessels of healing for hurting souls.

A hospital that advertised healing as its mandate but required everyone who passed through its doors to look and act healed would be worse than no hospital at all because it would not only deny healing to people, but it would remove hope of anyone finding healing. After all, one would think, 'if I can't receive healing in the one place that advertises it, then there's not really any healing anywhere'.

In the same way, a church that claims to offer emotional, spiritual or physical healing but does not want to have to deal with any of the realities of 'dis-ease' is worse than no church at all because it removes hope of finding healing. Perhaps that's why Paul told Timothy to *"have nothing to do with"* people who had a form of godliness but denied its power.

Unfortunately, many churches have become totally devoid of power. They endure year after year of stuffy services, never once expecting to see anything supernatural happen. They have no hope of God confirming His Word with signs and wonders following as He said He would do because they don't believe His Word. There is little faith found in either pew or pulpit. Everyone looks great - on the outside. I have noticed a curious thing. When 'Christians' in such churches meet, the conversation goes something like this: "Hi, how are you? You look wonderful!"

"I'm fine, thanks. You look great, too. I love your coat!"

"Oh thanks. You're looking younger every time I see you!"

"You're so sweet. Are you still playing squash?"

Ad nauseum. As though the major focus in life was to look good.

Christianity is not about social clubs. It is not about fashion shows. It is not about yuppie lifestyles. It is not a personality contest.

Christianity is about power - the power of the living God residing in redeemed human beings to free mankind from the evil which seeks to destroy each and every one of us. It is about the power in the Name of Jesus. It is about the power in the Word of God. It is about the power of the blood of Jesus.

It is about power resident in each of us who has the Spirit of Christ living within.

CHAPTER FIVE

LEARNING TO LISTEN TO THE HOLY SPIRIT

Dealing with the realm of spirits is not a natural thing to do. Very rarely does anyone ever see either an angel or a demon. Spirits generally cannot be perceived via our human senses and yet their influence upon us is massive. How does one deal with something that plays such a huge part in our lives and yet is beyond normal perception?

We have been given eyes to see everything that surrounds us in the natural realm. We know when it's time to cross the street because we can see that the light is green. We have ears to hear suggestions from others, praise, criticism, music, and fire alarms. With our fingertips we can identify objects and textures even when blindfolded. We are gifted with finely tuned sensory perceptions to cope with physical life on this planet.

TRIUNE CREATIONS

However, we are not merely physical beings. As triune creations, we are also emotional and spiritual creatures. We perceive situations of an emotional nature through something called intuition, an intangible but often dependable way of tuning in to those around us and of course no one has to be a Christian to have a highly developed sense of intuition.

EQUIPPED FOR LIFE

As our Creator, God did not leave us without resources in any aspect of our being. In order to cope in the realm of the spirits, we have been given the gifts of the

Holy Spirit. Some of these are gifts of revelation, some of power and some of utterance. 1 Corinthians 12:7-11 says, "*Now to each one the manifestation of the Spirit is given for the common good. To one there is given through the Spirit the message of wisdom, to another the message of knowledge by means of the same Spirit, to another faith by the same Spirit, to another gifts of healing by that one Spirit, to another miraculous powers, to another prophesy, to another distinguishing between spirits, to another speaking in different kinds of tongues, and to still another the interpretation of tongues. All these are the work of one and the same Spirit, and He gives them to each one, just as He determines.*"

SATAN'S COUNTERFEITS

Of course whatever God does, Satan counterfeits. That's why we have ESP, channelling, fortune tellers, witch doctors, Ouija boards, crystals, crystal balls, tarot cards, the demonic version of tongues, tea leaves etc. - all viable routes to contacting the spirit realm. The only problem is that they attract the wrong spirits.

While Satan encourages people to actually contact spirits, God's purpose in giving us the gifts of the Holy Spirit is to enable us to deal with the spiritual realm within the context of this physical world. Everyone wants to know the answers to the unknown. Who will I marry? Where can I find my stolen daughter? Will my wife come back to me? As Christians, we are warned against seeking any communication in the spiritual realm other than direct communication with God through Jesus Christ. God wants us to depend on Him and to trust Him for the future as well as the present. We can't possibly understand why God is allowing certain things in our lives and if we knew more than He wants us to know, we could sabotage His wonderful plan.

OPERATING IN THE GIFTS OF THE SPIRIT

In order to operate most effectively to further God's Kingdom, however, we need insight beyond our natural intuition. We need to know when to pray for angels to come to our assistance, what kind of spirits we are battling and whether the problems we encounter are spiritual or natural.

Ability to operate in the gifts of the Holy Spirit does not depend on any kind of natural talent, ability, Bible schooling or spiritual seniority. It simply depends upon sensitivity to the Spirit within, obedience to the urging of the Holy Spirit, devotion to God, desire to be used by Him and a willingness to look like an idiot if one is wrong.

While a brand new Christian can begin immediately to operate in the gifts of the Spirit, it takes time to learn to balance the operation of the gifts with wisdom. For instance, as one begins to move in the Word of Knowledge, God will impress certain things on his heart about individual people. If He shows me that someone is having an affair, it would ruin everything if I were to run to that person and say, "Aha, I know what you're doing. God told me that you are committing adultery!"

No. I would wait until the Holy Spirit gave me freedom to share with the person in a loving atmosphere. Just because God shows someone something about a person doesn't mean that He wants it blurted to the whole world right at that moment. He has simply given it ahead of time to put the sharer on standby alert to be sensitive to the proper timing to bring it forth.

ROAD BLOCKS

There are many people who say, "I would love to be able to hear God's voice, but He never speaks to me. I've never had any evidence of the gifts of the Holy Spirit in my life."

There are two major blocks to the movement of the Holy Spirit in a person's life. One is unbelief and the other is wrong theology.

Amazingly, a person who has either no or almost no background in the church and comes to know Christ will begin to move in the gifts of the Holy Spirit far more easily than a person who has been raised in an atmosphere of religious unbelief. Where blockages exist, if the person will pray and renounce unbelief or wrong teaching or what ever the blockage may be, the person will be set free to experience the moving of the Holy Spirit in his life.

THE FRUITS OF IGNORANCE

So often down through history the recorded method of dealing with the spiritual realm has been via ritual, mob hysteria, the occult or dependency upon human authorities - thus situations like the burning of witches in New England, voodoo charms or the practice of seeking out professional exorcists. None of these methods are scriptural.

HOW-TO

The Bible is basically a manufacturer's handbook, a how-to book for coping with every aspect of life. According to Scripture, anyone who believes can take authority over unclean spirits and command them to leave in the Name of Jesus. There's no formula, no required ritual, no props, no accreditation required beyond belief in Jesus and sensitivity to His Holy Spirit.

UNWRAPPING THE GIFTS

The gifts of the Spirit are the spiritual counterpart to our physical senses. They are critical in terms of being effective warriors in spiritual warfare. Let's take a brief look at each one.

The Word of Wisdom is the gift of having a word at the right time concerning a particular situation. It is having the right thing to say to a person at a critical moment, a supernatural word from the Lord in regard to a certain circumstance. It brings reassurance, not fear, and increases faith in the presence of the Lord.

A Word of Knowledge can allow us to discern the thoughts and intents of the hearts of others in certain circumstances. Thus it can take one directly to the cause of a problem. When one receives such a revelation from the Lord, it's important to persevere until the person responds, because people often need time to come into agreement with the word. As with all of the gifts, it's extremely important to seek confirmation in the body of believers. If it's from God, He will confirm His word.

The Gift of Faith comes from absolute belief in the Word of God and grows from reading Scripture constantly. In certain situations, the Holy Spirit will impress our hearts with illumination of a particular Scripture, a phenomenon called *rhema knowledge* in the original Greek. That illumination will pump us so full of faith that we will step out boldly in the knowledge that God is at work.

If one really believes Mark 16 where it says that believers will lay hands on the sick and they will be healed, then it follows that as we lay hands on sick people and pray for their recovery, healing begins immediately. Whether or not they receive the Gifts of Healing depends upon several complex factors. Some people don't want to be healed. Some don't believe in healing. Some are bound by spirits that have legal lodging in their beings and cannot experience God's healing until they are set free from things like bitterness, anger, unforgiveness, rejection, fear, etc. It is so important that God's love and compassion be ministered with Gifts of Healing.

The most prevalent problem associated with healing is that people with very low levels of belief lay their hands on others as part of the Christian 'thing' and they know in their hearts that nothing is going to happen because they don't really believe that God is going to do anything. Then, in order to justify themselves, they claim that the sick person doesn't have enough faith to receive healing or that the sin in their lives is blocking the healing. So many people have been devastated by submitting themselves to the hands of unbelievers for prayer.

The Gift of Miraculous Powers is often reflected in instantaneous healings. While gifts of healing may be manifested over a period of time, miraculous healings can happen in the blink of an eye.

Prophesy is for the edification, exhortation and encouragement of the Body - never for enlightenment. It is a very simple and beautiful gift. It may be a Scripture that God has given to be shared with the others present, or it may simply be a word of encouragement that He lays on one's heart to share. Most often, only a word or two will be given in the beginning, but as these are spoken forth in faith, the rest of the words will follow.

Distinguishing between Spirits is vital for Christian ministry. It relates to the recognition and removal of demons or evil spirits. While not everyone may have the ministry of deliverance, certainly every believer needs to know when to stand on the Word against evil powers in order to fight the spiritual warfare which we are all called to fight.

Speaking in different kinds of Tongues is an amazing gift. Sometimes, when God impresses upon us a great spiritual need, our cognitive understanding of the situation is foggy and we either don't know how to pray or we have no words suitable to express the depth of the need as we pray. In times like that, we need the Holy Spirit to pray through us and He does, in a language that we have never learned, a language that completely bypasses our own intellect and goes directly to the Father.

The Interpretation of Tongues is not necessarily a *translation* of a message in tongues. It may simply be an interpretation of the thought expressed in another language. Often people think that if the interpretation is not exactly of the same duration or pattern as the original tongue, it can't be the genuine thing. That's not necessarily true.

Obviously, the more that these gifts are evident through one's life, the more powerful one will be in spiritual ministry. The only way, however, to experience an increased flow of God's gifts through one to touch others is through increased yieldedness to Him. The more we seek the face of God through prayer, studying Scripture and worshipping Him, the greater will be our sensitivity to His voice directing our paths.

THE EARLY DAYS

When God first began to use my wife, Carmen, and me in setting people free from oppressing spirits, we didn't know much about the Gifts of the Spirit. We had never known anything but the structures of the Roman Catholic Church. At that time, for simple parishioners to begin praying deliverance over other parishioners was unheard of. Everyone thought that we had lost our senses - except the people who were being set free.

Although we were unschooled in Holy Spirit theology, we knew in our hearts that God was leading us. In spite of our confusion and concern we knew that we had to take what we had received and run with it. Good things were happening and we were excited. It took years before we really realized that God Himself had taught us and ordained our paths.

Recently, in sorting some old papers, I came across some notes that I made in those early days of ministry. It was a pattern for effective deliverance that I wrote down not long after the Lord began to use us in that capacity. Hiding the date it was written, I showed it to Carmen and asked her what she thought. She was very positive. When I revealed the date to her, she was dumbfounded. "How could we have known all that way back then?", she asked. We looked at each other in wonderment at how much the Lord Himself had taught us directly. I vividly recalled being in deep prayer one day and asking God specifically about how to set people free from the darkness in their lives. As thoughts filled my mind, I wrote them down and I'm so glad that I did.

FOUR NUGGETS

Essentially, God showed me four main points at that time which have for the most part remained the pattern for our ministry. Briefly, the four points are as follows:

1) Be sure of who you are in Christ before venturing into the unknown. A lukewarm Christian can find himself in serious danger through exercising his own bravado in dealing with the spirit realm. Acts 19:14 recounts the story of the seven sons of Sceva who tried to invoke the Name of Jesus as they attempted to drive out demons even though they did not know Jesus in any personal way. They simply tried

to use His Name on the basis of what they knew of Paul's ministry. Naturally, it didn't work and the demon turned on them and gave them all a good thrashing. Man on his own is powerless before Satan. However, Satan is powerless before a believer who confronts him covered by the blood of Jesus. Make sure that your life is right with God before beginning.

2) Before starting to pray, discuss the meaning and the consequences of the deliverance with the person who has come to you. Make him or her comfortable and remove any doubts or fears. Try to get some understanding of the things that are troubling him or her or may be causing concern. An atmosphere of safety, absolute confidentiality and love is paramount.

3) When you go into prayer, don't be in a rush. Stay before God for a good while before beginning to pray for deliverance. Invoke the Holy Spirit and the Blood of Jesus upon yourself and upon the person who is about to undergo deliverance. Remember that although Jesus gave us the power to cast out demons, it is the Spirit of Jesus within us who actually does the work. It's not us. It was He who paid the price. Not us. Know that God is with you and that the fact that you are acting in obedience to His Word assures you of His supernatural support. Continue to pray and to assure the person of the love and presence of Jesus and of the fact that Satan has been defeated and has no right to stay. He has no right to torment us unless we allow him to do so.

4) Before beginning to pray for deliverance, ask the person to renounce Satan and all of his works and powers. Encourage expression of his or her love for God and renunciation of the sin or sins that gave the spirit legal lodging with the person. Make sure that the person understands that unless he or she is

serious about repentance and is willing to change his or her lifestyle, it will be worse for the person after the deliverance than before. If a person is cleansed from evil but does not fill him or herself up with the Holy Spirit, the evil spirit will return and, finding the person empty, will bring seven spirits with him worse than himself, thus rendering the person into a worse state than he was in originally. Unless a person is willing to give up the lust of life, he will not be free.

One must love God more than the pleasure he or she derives from sin. This point in the deliverance is critical because it is very difficult to change habits and the person may need a lot of support. If the habit, lifestyle or sin that invited the spirit in in the first place is not changed, it would be much better for the person not to receive deliverance in the first place.

 THE FOUR STEP CHECK-UP

That was not all that the Holy Spirit taught us in those early days.

There were times when we did everything that we had been shown to do but saw no results. When we prayed for guidance, God showed us that we needed to do a four step check-up:

1) Examine our own faith. If our faith was weak and there was any sense of insecurity over whether or not we had the power to rout the demons, they would sense our lack of faith and stay put.

2) Make sure we weren't being fooled. Many times the spirit would come out but fool us into thinking that it was still there. If the believer's faith wavers, the spirit may simply return. Faith is dependent on believing, not on seeing. When the spirit is told to avlee in the Name of Jesus, we must believe, not hope or assume, but believe that it has gone.

3) Stop looking at the symptoms. The person

being prayed for may not feel any different following prayer and the symptoms may still be part of his or her behaviour patterning. It may take awhile for him or her to feel free or act normal but that does not mean that he or she has not been set free. If, however, the symptoms do not leave, it may be that the person has other spirits of the same family that haven't left. For instance, if a person has many spirits of fear, some may come out with deliverance while others continue to hide, thus keeping the host human bound in fear. It may be necessary to repeat the deliverance until *all* fear is gone.

Years ago when a friend of ours was living in the city, she had a huge dog that used to love to go for walks. Because of the urban surroundings, the dog was never allowed to run free, but because he had never known freedom, he was comfortable walking with a leash fastened to his collar. He used to love to hear the leash being taken down from the hook and got so excited when our friend would attach it to him. Eventually, she moved to the country where she set him free. He had miles he could roam if he wanted to. At first he stayed very close to the house. Eventually he began to explore a wider and wider circumference. However, the thing that made him most excited was when our friend would get the old leash out, fasten it to his collar again and take him for a walk. Old habits die hard. Being comfortable with the symptoms of bondage has nothing to do with the reality of having been set free.

4) Question the person. Was he sincere about giving up the things in his life that imprisoned him? Does he really want Jesus to be Lord of his life?

TESTING THE SPIRITS
We became very aware of the importance of the Gift of Discernment of Spirits.

1 John 4:1-3 tells us to test the spirits. It says, *"Dear friends, do not believe every spirit, but test the spirits to see whether they are from God, because many false prophets have gone out into the world. This is how you can recognize the Spirit of God: every spirit that acknowledges that Jesus Christ has come in the flesh is from God, but every spirit that does not acknowledge Jesus is not from God"*.

There's no point in asking if they believe in God, because of course they do, even though they tremble in his presence. Many demons believe a whole lot more heartily in God than some church going humans do. They know he's real. However, no demon spirit will say that Jesus is Lord because Jesus was the One who defeated them. To admit that Jesus came in the flesh means that they have to admit their defeat and if they do that, they know that they'll have to leave. Thus they resist admitting that Jesus is Lord.

The Gifts of the Spirit were given to the church. Had there not been problems with evil spirits in the church, there would have been no need to include the Gift of Discernment of Spirits in the gift basket. If our eyes could be opened just for a moment in a Sunday morning service in any church, I believe that we would be stunned at the activity that surrounds us. Spirits have no problem joining in singing praises to God. They are liars and simply worship a different god - Satan. But if they are challenged and asked to confess that Jesus is Lord, they will not.

DELIVERANCE IS A MINISTRY FOR THE CHURCH

I do not know one person in the deliverance ministry who feels that his ministry is to deliver the unsaved from demons. Let's face it. Deliverance is a ministry primarily for and to the church. It is one of the tools given to us to unwrap the grave clothes from those who are brought into new life in Christ.

The Holy Spirit taught us that deliverance is not an option. It is a must. If we are to fulfil the great commission and take the world for Christ, we must first bind the present power so that we can set the captives free. It can be a very difficult and dangerous ministry and must be taken very seriously. However, when God is for us, who can be against us?

When I look back on these notes from the days when we were taking our first baby steps, it amazes me that God loved us enough to teach us personally when no other teacher was available. Even today, when we are mindful of the content of these notes, people are gloriously set free and there is nothing more wonderful.

CHAPTER SIX

LET'S UNTANGLE THE CONFUSION

"I do not believe that a Christian can be demon possessed."

"She is definitely suffering from demonic depression."

"He is totally obsessed with violent movies."

"I feel so oppressed all the time."

"Something is definitely trying to repress my effectiveness. I can't get anywhere."

"Now, do you suppose that demon is inside her spirit, on her back, in her head or just plain harassing her from a two foot distance?"

In trying to sort out the roots of our problems, we have often appeared hopelessly entangled in confusion. Possession, oppression, obsession, depression, repression gobbledygook.

Paul speaks in Romans 7:22 of three levels within us. *"For I delight in the law of God, in **my inmost self**, but I see in **my members** another law at war with the law of **my mind** and making me captive to the law of sin which dwells in my members."*

I believe that Paul is referring to his *spirit* as his inmost self, his *body* as his members, and his *soul* as his mind. I do not believe that any true Christian can have his or her *inmost being* or *spirit* inhabited by a demon. That is the residence of the Holy Spirit and He will not share His place with another. We are purchased of God, bought with a very high price. Thus we are possessed by God. However, just as Paul speaks of another law in his body at war with the law of his mind, we are too often aware of the battle raging in our own lives between body and soul.

THE OPERATIVE WORD

The operative word is 'demonized'.

The Lord must get so tired of our idiocy. I would be a wealthy man if I had a nickel for every discussion I have heard in regard to the semantics of demonology. All anyone has to do is go to the Bible if he or she really wants answers.

The original Greek used only one word for demonic interference in the life of a Human. That word was *daimonizomai* and simply meant to be demonized, or under the influence of a demon or demons, whether to a greater or lesser degree. Some translations have erred in their assumption that demonization means possession. These translations have caused grave theological problems and great confusion where there does not need to be any confusion. The original Greek was very plain.

It's simple - no mystery. Scripture is very straight forward in its exposure of the dark kingdom. The main confusion regarding the topic is in the minds of people who allow themselves to be confused by Satan. As long as he can keep people endlessly discussing the subject, they won't be a threat to him. They can't act as long as they're debating.

 Possession, oppression, obsession, depression, and repression are all indicators of demonic activity - *daimonizomai* - and simply need to be dealt with as such. God knows all of the details in regards to how, where and why. If we had needed to know every particular, He would have spelled things out more clearly. He has given us as much as we need to know and directions for effectively overcoming the enemy.

GETTING IT RIGHT

When reading Scripture, it is extremely important to listen to the Holy Spirit for understanding. The Old

Testament was originally written in Hebrew and the New Testament was written in Greek. Given the imperfections of some translations, the liberties taken by paraphrasers and the differences in meaning of some words with the passing of the centuries, a true student of Scripture will be sure to work through the difficulties.

For instance, the King James Version translates Mark 10:14 as, *"Suffer the little children to come unto Me and forbid them not, for of such is the Kingdom of Heaven."* These days, the word 'suffer' implies pain. A reader unaware of changes with the passing of the centuries could conclude that Jesus wanted the little children to suffer in order to reach Him. Of course that is not the meaning at all. At the time of the original King James translation, the word 'suffer' meant 'to permit'. Jesus was indignant when the well-meaning disciples tried to block the children from entering freely into His presence and rebuked them. He subsequently took the little ones into His arms, put His hands on them and blessed them.

For purposes of clarification, the following words need to be understood in order to gain clear insight into the realm of the dark kingdom.

* *Demons* - powers of darkness, fallen angels.
* *Powers in the heavenlies* (Eph. 6:11) - demonic beings, fallen angels.
* *Rulers, powers, world forces of this darkness and spiritual forces of wickedness in the heavenly places* - Ephesians 6:12 outlines these four designations of Satan's highly organized dark kingdom. *"For our struggle is not against flesh and blood, but against the rulers, against the powers, against the world forces of this darkness, against the spiritual forces of wickedness in the heavenly places."*

* *Pergamum* - Satan's earthly headquarters, at the time John wrote the Revelation, located in the country we now call Turkey. (Revelation 2:12-13) It is interesting to note that that whole area is vehemently anti-Christian.

* *Dominions* (Eph. 6:11) - Territorial demons of authority. Rank of demons ruling nations, cities, towns.

* *Prince of the kingdom of Persia* - (Daniel 10:13) This was not an earthly prince, but a fallen angel or demonic ruler who controlled the Persian Empire. The angel who was sent from God to help Daniel but was delayed, said, *"But the prince of the kingdom of Persia was withstanding me for twenty-one days; then, behold, Michael, one of the chief princes, came to help me, for I had been left there with the kings of Persia."* Each earthly nation has its corresponding spiritual counterpart in Satan's highly structured organization. These are ruled by powerful spiritual forces who seek to keep people from the blessings of God and carry out the agenda of their evil master, Satan.

* *Omnipresent* - Only God is omnipresent, present everywhere all of the time. Satan is limited to only one geographical location at any one time. (Job 1:6,7) It is only through the network of his demonic hosts that he is able to be active worldwide.

* *Demon possessed* - a person who is owned by Satan, not born again by the Spirit of God.

* *Demonized* - a person who is influenced by demons, whether in or on the person. Can be either Christian or non-Christian.

* *Angels* - Created beings of spiritual nature.

* *Fallen angels* - became demons. (Satan is a fallen angel.) Revelation 12:4 says, *"And his (the great*

red dragon's) tail swept away a third of the stars of Heaven and threw them to the earth.". According to Jude 6, some of these angels have already been confined, while others of them are still very active in the world.

* *Morning Star* - title given to Jesus. Satan the counterfeiter often appears *as* the morning star to deceive people.

UNTANGLE THE ROOT OF THE PROBLEM

Defeated Christians are usually confused Christians. They wallow in their unhappy circumstances, feeling as though every step they take is through four feet of mud in heavy combat boots.

They have allowed Satan to confuse them as to the root of their unhappiness.

They see their husbands, wives, debts, or whatever as their enemies, when their actual enemies are either Satan or their own flesh (meaning bad habits, sloppiness, wrong desires, negative attitudes or whatever).

Victorious Christians are people who dare to stop blaming other people and circumstances for their unhappiness. They change what they are able to change and confront Satan to take back anything that he may be trying to steal from them.

COMMON QUESTIONS

So many people have come to us with questions. The following are a few of our answers to those most often asked.

Q. Do angels have ranks and territories?
A. Some do. For instance, we're told in Daniel 10 that Michael is a prince among the angels. He is responsible for the nation of Israel.

Q. What about powers and principalities? Are there certain demons with rank that rule over certain areas?
A. Again in the tenth chapter of Daniel we read about an angel who was sent to minister to Daniel. After Daniel had been fasting for twenty-one days, the angel finally came to him, having struggled with the prince of the Persian Kingdom for the whole three weeks, from the first day of Daniel's fast.

This prince was apparently a demon exercising powerful influence over the Persian realm in the interests of Satan. Michael, one of the chief angels finally had to come to the assistance of the angel who had been sent to minister to Daniel and rout the enemy.

Obviously, some demons are more powerful than some angels. Some angels are more powerful than others and some demons are more powerful than other demons. Just as God's Kingdom is highly organized, so is the dark kingdom organized into ranking demons with specific geographic locations of influence.

Q. Can a Christian be demon possessed?
A. No. Possession denotes ownership. Christians are owned by Jesus. They have been bought with a price and can therefore not be possessed by Satan. Unfortunately, the words 'possessed' and 'demonized' mean the same things in the minds of many people.

Q. Can a Christian be demonized or under the influence of a demon?
A. Yes. In actual fact, very few people are not demonized. They are the ones who are able to acutely discern demonic suggestions and interference and overcome through the blood of the Lamb. In truth, a very small percentage of Christians are over comers. Most

Christians "wrestle not" and are consequently under the influence of demons much of the time. Thus the problems within churches of overeating, alcohol abuse, marital problems, teenage rebellion, strange beliefs, etc. When Christians are set free, these things are not problems in their lives.

Q. If a Christian is demonized, does that mean that a demon controls his mind?
A. Not necessarily. Demons regularly offer temptations to people. The process of being tempted is a stage of demonization.

However, simply being harassed or tempted does not mean that we lose control. Because control of our minds is ours to keep or to submit to either God or Satan, we can fall into the trap of coming into agreement with Satan in our minds in regard to a particular temptation.

For example, if a demon suggests to a married woman that a particular man is desirable, she can either recognize the source of the suggestion as ungodly and take authority over it (usually over and over again until the thought no longer brings sensuous feelings), or she can agree with the suggestion in her mind and enjoy the feelings under the illusion that no harm is being done. When she chooses to entertain the feelings, she gives Satan legal entry to her mind and he very happily sends an unclean spirit which takes control. The woman then loses control of those thoughts and cannot stop thinking about the man. They become so strong that she cannot resist acting on the thoughts either by approaching the man or somehow bringing destruction down on her head - unless she repents, resists Satan and goes to God for release.

Q. I thought that Salvation brought cleansing of the mind. Why does Paul urge Christians in Romans 12:1,2 to "renew" their minds?

A. In this passage, Paul urges the brethren to offer their bodies as living sacrifices, holy and pleasing to God as a spiritual act of worship. He says, *"Do not conform any longer to the pattern of this world, but be transformed by the renewing of your mind"*.

He is making it clear that our bodies are the most valuable properties that we have. Since they are not yet redeemed and yet have been bought through the shed blood of Jesus, we are called to take charge of our bodies and sacrifice our natural desires to the will of God.

In the same way, the transformation of the mind depends on a radical act of our wills which results in renewed minds. Although the spirit of a Christian is redeemed, his mind remains subject to temptations of the flesh. However, unless the mind is free, it is very difficult to relax and enjoy the abundant life Jesus promised.

Q. 2 Corinthians 5:17 says that, "if anyone is in Christ, he is a new creation; the old has gone, the new has come". If we are new creations, how can we still be troubled and influenced by demons?

A. In this passage, Paul is referring to the spirit as new, not the body or the soul. In Romans 8:23, he speaks of the inward groaning of every Christian as we eagerly await the redemption of our bodies.

While our spirits are instantly redeemed when we repent and accept Christ, we live in an unredeemed world with unredeemed bodies and unredeemed souls. In John 3:3, Jesus speaks of being 'born again'. As Nicodemus observed, a second birth cannot have physical meaning. It is a spiritual phenomenon. In the same way, Paul's reference to the 'new creation' pertained to the spiritual condition of man. At the moment of spiritual birth, our old bodies still ache and our personalities still bear mute witness to the winds of circumstance that have formed us. Our bodies and our minds are native to Planet Earth and can be vulnerable to the influence of its ruler - Satan.

Q. *If Scripture says that we have been given the mind of Christ, how can our souls be unredeemed?*
A. Although 1 Corinthians 2:16 is glorious in its affirmation that "we have the mind of Christ", it is our responsibility to make sure that we retain godliness. Without a firm grip on our resolve, our minds can fall prey to anything. Having the mind of Christ means having a new sensitivity to what is acceptable or not acceptable to God. We recognize sin and become acutely aware of the importance of not sinning. However, if we harden ourselves against submission to His Spirit, we can be given over to reprobate minds. 2 Corinthians 10:5 warns us to "*take captive every thought to make it obedient to Christ*". Unless we do this, we will be tossed to and fro at the whim of Satan and his dark troops.

Q. *But if we become children of God and move from the realm of darkness into light when we become Christians, how can we continue to be demonized if God our Father has control over Satan?*
A. In spite of the fact that we have been reborn spiritually, we live in fleshly bodies in a carnal world where Satan legally has dominion. In the seventh chapter of Romans, Paul makes it clear that as Christians, we have to struggle against forces that we neither understand nor want. "*For what I want to do I do not do, but what I hate, I do. And if I do what I do*

not want to do, I agree that the law is good. As it is, it is no longer I myself who do it, but it is sin living in me. I know that nothing good lives in me, that is, in my sinful nature. For I have the desire to do what is good, but I cannot carry it out."

Satan was present in our bodies and souls before we allowed Jesus to purchase our spirits. He remains there unless we consistently claim every aspect of our beings for the Lord Jesus Christ.

Q. How can one tell the difference between works of the flesh and works of Satan or his demon powers?
A. The two are closely linked, but the difference is generally a matter of degree. For instance, Galatians 5:19-21 outlines the works of the flesh which include immorality, impurity, debauchery, idolatry, witchcraft, hatred, discord, jealousy, fits of rage, selfish ambition, envy, etc. While these things can be present without demonization in the life of any person who is not entirely yielded to the Holy Spirit, they can be open doors for the entry of evil spirits if we continue in them.

For instance, a person who regularly allows him or herself to indulge in fits of anger without trying to control him or herself may unknowingly open the door for a spirit of anger to enter.

Q. I've heard a little bit about transference of spirits. Is it common for a spirit coming out of a person during deliverance to fasten itself to someone nearby as it is cast out of the first person?
A. It can happen. That is why we pray for the protection of the Blood of Jesus on everyone present before we pray deliverance. However, fear is overcome by faith. We have to fix our eyes on victory over evil. We must be bold, knowing that the enemy cannot

stand before the Name of Jesus. If we quake in fear over something the enemy might try to do, we are in the wrong place. He can do only what we allow him to do.

Q. *When you command an evil spirit to come out of someone, where do you tell it to go? I've heard people send them to the foot of the cross. Is that correct?*
A. Matthew 12:43 says, "*When an evil spirit comes out of a man, it goes through arid places seeking rest and does not find it.*" We simply tell the spirits to go where Jesus tells them to go. I don't see any scriptural directive for them to be sent to the cross or into the deep or anywhere other than dry places.

Q. *Can I pray for someone who is far away to be delivered of a demon?*
A. Certainly you can. Jesus is the deliverer and He is not limited by time or space. He is omnipresent by His Holy Spirit. However, we have found far greater success when we pray with people face to face. It is very important to have the cooperation of the person for whom you are praying. People generally need to be led through repentance and forgiveness in order to shake the spirits loose.

Q. *I thought that Jesus put angels in charge of us. Why should we have to worry?*
A. It's true. He did. However, don't be fooled into forgetting that Satan as the counterfeiter tries to put demons in charge of us whenever he can.

Q. *How about crystals and channelling?*
A. So many people are fooled just because they get accurate details from the occult. Don't forget that

demons don't die. They have been around since the beginning of the earth and they are privy to every detail of history. They can conjure up anything you want to know about the past and they have no conscience about lying about the future.

Q. There's a lot being written about past lives and reincarnation. Sometimes it's hard to reject some of the evidence. What do you think?
A. I don't think; I know, because God's Word, which is our authority, claims that *"man is destined to die once and after that to face judgment"* (Hebrews 9:27). What actually happens is that demons hop from generation to generation. They carry with them details of the lives of people they inhabited in past generations. Thus it is not the people themselves who have the memories; it is the spirits that inhabit them. This is actually a very powerful tool of Satan's because by imparting false memories to people, he fools them into doubting Scripture.

Q. We're hearing more and more about Multiple Personality Disorder. Does that have anything to do with demons?
A. Anyone who has studied Psychology knows that the brain can suffer distortion. However, I believe that many of the mental aberrations we confront are actually situations of demonization.
Many so called cases of MPD are not separate personalities of one person but individual spirits disguising themselves within that person. If not, why is it when supposed fragmentation occurs that curses and profanity abound while praises to God are not evident? From our experience, many apparent mental disorders can be most successfully approached through deliverance.

CHAPTER SEVEN

CHARACTERISTICS OF DEMON SPIRITS

We have known Mike for a good number of years. When we first met him, he was a born again Christian man who attended church regularly and studied the Word with his family. He appeared to be an average sort of fellow, pleasant to meet and certainly not the type one would consider strange or offensive at first meeting. He was a highly gifted artist, capable of creating extraordinary designs. He was not, however, as we came to discover, warmly welcomed into the social fabric of the Christian community. No one appreciated his insistence on having the last word in every discussion nor his quarrelsome nature when things didn't go exactly his way.

It was a well known fact that Mike's sporadically pleasant public face masked a Jekyll and Hyde personality that played havoc with his family. Despite his desire to be a good father and husband, he had a vicious temper that could flare with neither warning nor provocation.

Everyone in his house lived on the edge, fearing the sudden reemergence of the monster Mike could be. Times of peace within the home were marred by the resentment everyone held toward him for the inconsistency of his love. No one could relax while he was there.

Mike was not a happy man. He sincerely wanted to live a solid Christian life but just when it would seem that he was beginning to get on track, something would come over him and he would lose control. He found himself driven to draw macabre scenes of sadistic horror and his strange sexual desires were deeply embarrassing to both Mike and his wife. He sometimes wondered if he was losing his mind.

One day Mike was talking to a man who had come to us for prayer about some difficulties he had been having. As they chatted, the man felt impressed to suggest to Mike that he, too, should try prayer.

Encouraged, Mike made an appointment and came to see us. As Carmen and I and a member of our prayer team prayed and asked the Lord to be with us in the meeting, we asked Him to protect us with the blood of Jesus and we commanded any unholy spirits that might be present to be bound in obedience to the Lord Jesus Christ.

Suddenly, Mike was thrown violently to the floor and began to make lunging movements toward us as he attempted to get up and attack us. However, because we had bound the spirits, he was unable to get up. As we asserted our authority, the spirits began to quiet down and Mike was able to get up from the floor and back into his chair. When he had recovered his composure we proceeded to ask him a few questions in an effort to establish the root of his problems.

The first thing we touched on was the occult, asking about any possible involvement. He admitted that he had been fascinated with it ever since his youth.

As a boy he had experienced the anguish of loneliness and insecurity living in an unstable home with very proud parents who never affirmed his worth. He had begun to grasp at unnatural straws to fill the void within.

One route he had taken was experimentation with ritualistic killing of animals, feeling that their death gave him power. During those early years he had often escaped from reality into fantasy daydreams where he dwelt as a powerful being who travelled far and wide in absolute conquest over all who would dare to face him.

He developed an intense aversion to crucifixes and whenever possible, he desecrated them in the most foul way.

One day as he fantasized about a particular situation, he found it all happening in reality. He began to discover an amazing power within him to think something and then have it happen. For instance, if he wanted to meet a friend, he could just think of a place in his mind that he wanted to meet him, go there and actually find the friend.

For awhile, Mike was very excited about his new powers. However, things began to happen in his home that were out of the realm of either his imagination or his control. Objects began to move around apparently on their own. He began to see people who he had known but who had died, walking in and out of his home. Animals would growl and run away when he approached them. He knew that something very strange was happening to him and he began to fear for his life.

In spite of the odd occurrences which had become very much part of his life by the time we met Mike, he was able to function on the surface as a relatively normal person.

Carmen and I began to delve into his knowledge and conviction of Christ, his conversion and his Christian walk. From what he said, it was apparent that he was indeed a born-again believer. I decided to test the spirits.

Although we do not always anoint people with oil prior to praying with them, I felt led to this time. I had not mentioned my intentions to either the rest of the prayer team or Mike. There was no way he could have known what I was doing when I got up to get the oil. He could not have seen it because I had to go behind a partition to get it and yet as I reached for the bottle, he called, "No oil, no oil. I don't want to be anointed with oil!" In spite of his protestations, I approached him with the bottle and he jumped up as if to run out of the office. We commanded him to sit down and he did.

As I proceeded to anoint Mike with the oil, Carmen got up to get a cross from a drawer. Although we never use crosses in a deliverance, we wanted to test his reaction to it after having heard of his aversion to crucifixes. Once again, he could not have had any idea of what Carmen was getting and yet he warned us to keep the cross away from him before she even brought it out!

As we prayed, Mike expressed deep repentance for his involvement in the occult and other ungodly attitudes and activities. In response to his desire to be free from everything in his life that was not of God, we proceeded to bind the spirits and to command them to tell us who they were. One by one, they named themselves. There were demons of the occult, lust, hatred, anger, unforgiveness, violence, control and many others. I demanded to know the name of the ruling power and lust came forward.

As I commanded it to leave, a raging battle began within Mike. We could see hatred for us burning in his eyes as he struggled to leave. However, because we had bound the spirits he could not move and so he simply spewed forth a venomous volley of threats. Thank God for His protection or we would have all been in mortal danger. I couldn't help thinking of the seven sons of Sceva in the Bible who attempted to cast out demons without the personal protection of Jesus. They didn't fare too well.

 However, the power in the Name of Jesus was more than enough to control the demons we were facing.

When the spirit of lust finally realized that the jig was almost up and it was going to have to leave, it tried a new tack. In a seductive, authoritative voice it attempted to convince us to let it stay. Motioning Mike's hand toward me as an indication of its desire to speak specifically with me, it asked, "What do you want from me? Why are you bothering me?".

Refusing to engage in any discussion, I simply continued to command it to leave in the Name of Jesus.

In the manner of a business person attempting to negotiate a deal, it continued, "Do you want money? Fame? Tell me what you want in life and I will get it for you, even more than you desire. Just ask me."

Again I paid no attention to its words but continued to demand its departure as the prayer team praised and worshipped God.

It tried another approach. "Don't you understand that I need this body? How am I going to satisfy myself without a body?"

These questions confirmed my belief that demon spirits need human bodies for the fulfilment of their particular personalities or characteristics. However, still refusing to negotiate, I continued to remind it that it had to obey and leave when commanded to do so in the Name of Jesus.

In abject desperation it cried, "It is so dark, so dry out there. Please understand that I need this body. You just don't understand how much I need this body. It's so dry, so uncomfortable, so painful out there!"

Ignoring the pleas, we continued to speak the Name of Jesus. By this time, Mike had been lying on the floor for some time. Suddenly, he jumped up with a grotesquely menacing expression and lunged at us. Before he could touch us, however, he fell back on to the floor, sobbing, groaning, sometimes grunting like a wounded animal.

It was obvious that unseen forces were battling hard to maintain ground that they already knew was lost to them.

As Mike's will to be free finally broke the remnants of the enemy power, he at last sighed a deep breath of release and totally relaxed. With tears in his eyes he slowly stood up and said, "It is gone. I felt a pressure leaving me and I know that I am free."

As we sat and chatted for awhile, Mike apologized for his behavior and explained that he had simply been a helpless spectator in the whole process. Although he had been aware of everything that was happening, he had had no power to overcome the thing that controlled him. Over and over again, he said, "It wasn't me. It wasn't me. I heard myself talking, but it wasn't me. I had no control over my body."

After thanking God for His mercy, we told Mike that there were possibly still some demon spirits hiding out, hoping to stay unnoticed. He understood and agreed to return a week later for more prayer.

The following week, the same three of us welcomed Mike once more. No sooner had we begun to pray and worship God in the Name of Jesus than Mike fell on the floor and once again began to challenge us, demanding to know what we wanted of him.

Once again we commanded the spirits to name themselves. Sure enough, more spirits of the occult and violence came forward. They proceeded to tell us that they were not going because they had been there for a long time. Mike's body was their home and besides, Mike needed them. Without them, they claimed, he was nothing but a helpless human.

We reminded the spirits of who we were and that we had the power in the Name of Jesus to cast them out. We bound them, rendering them powerless, until such time as they should leave. Of course threats and denials continued to come from them, but when we asked Mike why he was on the floor, the spirits responded that it was because they had been bound. Nevertheless, they refused to leave.

It took some patience and a lot of steadfast determination that no demon spirit could stay and continue to demonize Mike when ordered to leave in the Name of Jesus before the entire demonic force finally left.

To see Mike now totally free to be the person he always wanted to be, a loving family man and a gifted painter, serving the Lord Jesus with all of his heart, is sufficient to make anyone weep with gratitude to the great Deliverer.

We learned a lot about the characteristics of demon spirits through Mike's experience and through other deliverances in which we have been involved.

Demons have feelings and emotions. - Their emotions are counterfeits of humans. While some of their desires are like human desires, they are entirely perverted in motivation and behaviour. James 2:19 says, *"You believe that God is one. You do well; the demons also believe, and shudder."* The word, 'shudder' in Greek means, "to bristle, to shiver, to have the hair on end". It is very apparent during deliverance sessions that demons are very fearful of believers. They know that they will lose their places of refuge if they are discovered and cast out.

They are profoundly selfish. They seek only to please themselves with no regard for the problems they impose upon humans. Their mission is to steal, kill and destroy.

Demon spirits are ruthless. They stop short of nothing to fulfil their perverted, abominable desires.

They are proud. The fall of Satan and one third of the angels was a consequence of pride. Satan wanted the

worship which was due only to God. When his igno-
minious defeat shattered his wicked fantasies of
usurping God, he and his troops determined to overtake
the next best thing - humans who are made in the
image of God.

They need bodies. Although demon spirits have
emotions and drives, they are unable to express and
fulfil themselves without the use of human bodies.
They seem to be vagabond spirits who drift about in
extreme discomfort in dry places and who can find rest
only through finding a receptive human body (Matthew
12: 43-44).

Once they are discovered and routed, they may
wander for awhile in the dry places, but if they don't
find another host body right away, they will return
with other evil spirits (in order to bolster their strength)
to their former place and try to re-enter.

If they find that the body is not being kept filled with
the Holy Spirit, the original spirit will re-enter with its
allies and the person will be far worse off than he or she
was prior to the original deliverance. That is why it is
so important to follow up any deliverance with counselling and Christian encouragement. That is also why
it is not only pointless, but heartless to deliver a non-
believer.

They are deceptive liars. Satan is called the father of
lies. There is no truth in any demon. That is one reason
why it is so important not to converse with any spirit
other than the Holy Spirit. The frightening thing is that
while people imagine themselves to be in control of
themselves as they go on their way fulfilling their
lustful desires, they are blinded to the fact that they are
simply puppets on strings, complying with the evil
suggestions planted in their minds by deceptive
demonic forces who seek to fulfil their own lustful
cravings via unredeemed human bodies. Thus hu-

mans unknowingly lend their bodies for the pleasure of demons. Worse still, an ungodly sex partner may be totally blinded to the fact that he or she is actually having sex with a demon.

While Satan himself has no interest in fulfilling the lusts of the lower nature, he allows his demon spirits to gratify themselves, perhaps partly as payment for their services in helping him to realize his agenda. Satan's focus is victory over God, any way he can get it.

He tries to keep people from the knowledge of God's Word, because once they know that God offers freedom from pain and torment, Satan's place is lost.

They love to control individuals and nations. Once a demon is allowed a foothold, it proceeds to exert absolute control in the particular area of its specialty. For instance, demons of lust will control the sexual appetites of their victims.

The fruit of their presence is torment. The thoughts that fill the mind of a demonized person will be tormented in whatever areas the resident demons control.

Individual demons are recognizable by the characteristics of the evil tasks they wish to perform. For instance, a lying spirit will manifest its presence in a person's life by influencing him or her to lie over and over again.

A spirit of low self esteem will make a person feel and act as though he or she has no worth.

Sexual demons such as incubus (demons manifesting male likeness to female victims) and succubus (demons manifesting seductive female likeness to male victims) seduce vulnerable humans to indulge in actual intercourse with the demon.

Sexual seduction is high on Satan's list of priorities because he knows that the human body of a believer is the temple of the Holy Spirit (I Cor. 3:16) and he seeks to defile God's dwelling place. He knows that a person who commits adultery destroys him/herself (Proverbs 6:32). That is why our planet is flooded with polluted whirlpools and rapids of smutty T.V., magazines, novels, movies, videos etc., all designed to sweep the Bride of Christ right into Hell.

Demons are no respecters of persons. Any person, rich or poor, healthy or lame, black or white, old or young, believer or pagan is fair game as long as a door to the body is open or unguarded. In Matthew 15:22 we read about a Canaanite woman who had worshipped idols, who asked Jesus to set her daughter free from a demon. Because of her faith, Jesus honoured her request.

In the 13th Chapter of Luke we have the story of a believer, a good woman who Jesus called a "daughter of Abraham". She had been bound by Satan for 18 years, bent over, totally incapable of straightening her spine, until Jesus delivered her of her infirmity.

They are abusive. Demons care only about fulfilling their own evil desires and could care less about the harm they do to humans in the process. They may be abusive on every level - physically, emotionally and spiritually. As a matter of fact, I believe that the reason why Jesus honoured the request of the evil spirits in the demonized man to enter the pigs, was because of His concern for the abuse that the spirits would inflict upon the man as they were wrenched loose from him, unless He allowed them to enter the bodies of the pigs rather than thrusting them from their home into dry places.

They have a will of their own. It was Lucifer's self-will rebelling against God's will that started the whole problem. According to Isaiah 14:13,14, he said,

> " I will ascend to Heaven.
>   I will raise my throne above the stars.
>   I will sit on the mount of assembly.
>   I will ascend above the heights of the clouds.
>   I will make myself like the Most High."

Matthew 12: 43-44 says, *"Now when the unclean spirit goes out of a man, it passes through waterless places, seeking rest, and does not find it. Then it says, 'I will return to my house from which I came'* ". Like Satan, demons make their own decisions about what they are going to do. It is not uncommon for a stubborn demon to refuse to leave a human during a deliverance session insisting, "I will not go! This is my home and I'm staying here!".

Of course no matter how strong willed they may be, they eventually have to submit to the victory of Christ and depart according to the Word. That is why it is so important to persevere in deliverance and never to take "no" for an answer from a demon.

They are inventive. Demons are malevolently creative in their attempts to get a hold on the lives of people. They are very sneaky, promising fun and happiness but paying up with pain.

They are very cold and calculating. Demons know exactly what they want and they go after it in a methodical manner.

They are absolutely merciless. They drive people to madness with no conscience. We have come across many people who hear clear voices telling them to do terrible things like murdering themselves or others. No matter how disgusted the host humans may be by some of the thoughts that besiege them, the tormentors continue to pound away at them, day after day, with unthinkable thoughts.

They are divisive. Because unity in believers, families, individuals and geographical areas is so counterproductive to the work of Satan, division is one of his primary focuses. Through planting destructive thoughts in people's minds, he creates distrust not only among people, but toward God.

Demons can speak. Mark 3:11,12 records an instance where demons spoke to Jesus and were then commanded not to make his presence known. *"And whenever the unclean spirits beheld Him, they would fall down before Him and cry out, saying, 'You are the Son of God!' And He earnestly warned them no to make Him known."* It is very common for demons to take control of a person's vocal chords during deliverance. For instance, a normally gentle person may speak in an arrogant, abusive manner, thus revealing the intruder within.

They are aware of their own individuality, function and names. In Mark 5:7-9 when Jesus confronted the demonized man and subsequently commanded the demons to leave him and go into a herd of pigs, the spirit told Jesus that its name was Legion and that there were many demons in the man. Demons are not simply indistinct forces affecting human lives. Each is a living, totally corrupt being, with the mission of fulfilling Satan's evil purposes. They are out to destroy the divine likeness of man to God.

They are entirely aware of the reality of God and His omnipotent supremacy. *"And just then there was in their synagogue a man with an unclean spirit; and he cried out, saying, "What do we have to do with You, Jesus of Nazareth? Have You come to destroy us? I know who You are - the Holy One of God!"* (Mark 1:23,24). Citizens of the dark kingdom are far more aware of the reality of God than man is. Unredeemed man is blinded from the truth of God by Satan because man's knowledge of the Holy One puts Satan and his evil forces in mortal danger.

Acts 19:15 records another example of demons' knowledge of God and His Kingdom. *"And the evil spirit answered and said to them, 'I recognize Jesus, and I know about Paul, but who are you?'"* The spirits are very aware of the spiritual state of individuals.

Of course this is just a very light sketch of the characteristics of demons. Whatever negative characteristics one can imagine as possible for man are realities as characteristics of evil spirits.

CHAPTER EIGHT

OPERATION OF THE DARK KINGDOM

"The Devil made me do it!" Remember Flip Wilson and his line that became an acceptable comedic excuse for every transgression on Planet Earth?

Satan loved that line even more than Flip did. It catapulted him right out of the realm of reality into comedy routine fantasy.

From the very first encounter Satan had with humans in the Garden of Eden, his modus operandi was disguise. Because the hearts of Adam and Eve were pure before the fall, there was no evil within them upon which to build. He had to approach them externally. Because there were at that time no other humans on earth, he had to use the agency of an inferior creature through which to exert his slimy influence. He chose to appear to them as a magnificent serpent.

Most major Bible commentaries agree that the early serpents were probably far superior in beauty and sagacity to what they are in their present state. Because serpents are proverbial for wisdom (Matt.10:16), the disguise worked well in permitting Satan to work within its character as he articulated crafty suggestions to Eve. *"Did the Lord really say you must not eat from any tree in the garden?"* (Genesis 3:1) For the first time in her storybook life, Eve doubted God.

The scary part of the account of the fall of mankind was the fact that Eve had been in perfect unity with God. She had walked in the Spirit in a way that must have been awesome - and yet, when Satan masqueraded as an angel of light (II Cor. 11:14), offering to lead her to the true interpretation of God's words, Eve did not question Satan, but naively (stupidly) accepted him as a heavenly messenger. Had an observer been there, he or she might have intervened, saying, "Eve, wake up! Snakes don't talk. You're being deceived!" Of course Scripture tells us that Adam was right there, but like many husbands, he seemed to be paying absolutely no attention to his wife. Like many husbands, he lived to deeply regret his preoccupation with other things.

If Eve, who knew God in a way no one has known Him since the fall, was so easily deceived, how much more do we, who see through a glass so darkly, need to be on guard?

Unfortunately, in spite of Adam's physical presence, Eve was somehow on her own at the time, as we often are when Satan or his cohorts plant evil suggestions or thoughts into our minds. Adam may have simply been nearby. As Eve pondered Satan's question, it intrigued her and she entered into conversation with the one who had questioned God, thereby opening herself up to suggestion from the evil one.

Satan's suggestions were appealing. Had Eve refused to listen to him from the beginning, history (and her story) would have been quite different.

However, Eve not only listened and responded, she invited Satan's commentary on God's instructions. This gave Satan legal right to input his agenda into Eve's thought processes. What he gave her was a black and white contradiction of what she knew to be right. One would think at this point that a person who knew God as intimately as Eve did would clue in.

Perhaps she did. Nonetheless, by this time, she had opened herself completely to the idea of trying the forbidden fruit and every fibre of her being was saying, "Yes! I've got to taste it!" Any apprehension she may have had was being stuffed way down under the delicious anticipation of 'doing it'.

And so what happened? Eve had a great treat. The fruit was just as yummy as it had appeared on the tree. As her teeth penetrated the sun kissed skin and sank into the sweet, juicy flesh of the fruit, the citrus nectar flooded her taste buds with pure delight. She called Adam over and said, "Oh, Adam, try this. You've got to take a bite. This is the best thing I've ever tasted!"

Scripture does not record one teeny tiny gesture of resistance from Adam. At least Eve gave her rebellion a bit of thought. She discussed it before caving in. Not Adam. He just took that thing and dug right in. What was wrong with these people?

Immediately, Scripture says, their eyes were opened (Genesis 3:7).

Where was the serpent now? He was still there, as smug and brazen as he could be. He had won a big prize. Far be it from him to slither into obscurity when he could hang around and gloat. This was his first effort to draw humans away from God and it worked so well that he has used exactly the same formula ever since:

1. Find an area of weakness.
2. Present an outward object of attraction related to the weakness.
3. Influence an inward commotion of the subject's mind.
4. Increase passionate desire for the object to the point of triumph.
5. Stand back and laugh at the degradation, slavery and ruin of the subject's soul.

Adam and Eve's pleasure in sin was intense, but over, in the blink of an eye. Never, after that initial bite, did they ever have the opportunity to taste of the fruit of that tree again. Not only was the object of their desire denied them, but they lost their relationship with God.

121

LIKE JUDAS WHO NEVER SPENT A DIME.

They became mortal. They lost their home, their heritage, their ministry and their innocence. They reaped pain, frustration, labour, guilt and misery and plunged all of their posterity into the same painful abyss.

SATAN'S COUNTERFEITS

Satan often counterfeits what God does. Where God promises to work all things together for good to those that love Him and are called according to His purposes (Romans 8:28), Satan takes the sin of an individual and uses it like yeast to work through every aspect of the person's life, internally and externally, ruining not only his or her life, but aspects of the lives of surrounding friends, family, coworkers etc., thereby working all things together for sorrow to those who listen to him. No one ever sins in a vacuum.

God has given gifts to his children (I Cor. 12:8-10) which are to be used as encouragement, exhortation or edification but never for enlightenment. These fall into three categories. There are gifts of revelation, gifts of power and gifts of utterance. Satan, too, gives supernatural gifts but their purpose is always confusion, enslavement or a kind of enlightenment that is called an abomination to God in Leviticus 18 and Deuteronomy 18.

God's gifts	Sata's counterfeits
message of wisdom	astrology
message of knowledge	horoscope - necromancy
gift of faith	divination - superstition
gift of healing	occult healing
miraculous powers	occult powers - charms
prophesy	fortune telling - palmistry, tea leaves

discernment of spirits	familiar spirit - channelling
tongues	false tongues - spirit talk
interpretation of tongues	false interpretation

People have a natural curiosity about what lies ahead. It is a weakness common to man. Satan's counterfeits are designed to titillate and tease the hunger for knowledge about the future, giving just enough hints and promises to keep his followers addicted. He never fulfils a hunger, he simply creates more hunger.

Over and over again through Scripture we see God working through Spiritual music in battle and in times of peace to strengthen and encourage His people and to give them a vehicle through which they can praise and worship Him (I Kings 3:15, I Samuel 16:23). It is no secret that Satan, too, works through his personal brand of music. His beat churns through the soul and arouses ungodly responses in every fibre of the flesh. His lyrics are daily becoming more and more brazen, exposing his purposes to steal, kill and destroy. He encourages suicide, euthanasia, rebellion and abuses of every kind.

Where God has given us plants and herbs for food and the healing of our bodies, Satan has taken God's creation and refined, combined and processed certain plants as drugs with no purpose but destruction of humanity. When people are under the influence of drugs, they can't think clearly or normally. Thus it is impossible for them to respond to God out of any sense of reality. The only way it can happen is through a sovereign act of God clearing their minds, usually in response to some concerned person's prayers.

Satan even counterfeits religion. In 2 Timothy 3:4, Paul speaks of people in the last days who, "*have a form of godliness but deny its power*". He warns

Timothy to have nothing to do with these people. Stop and think about this for a moment. How many people do you know who go to church every Sunday but pay no attention to the Supernatural aspects of the Christian message? Do you have friends who don't expect answers to their prayers (if they indeed ever bother to pray)? Do you have friends who don't expect to see people healed by God? Do you have friends who scoff at the very idea of speaking in tongues? Paul would have told you to stay away from them. Religious spirits run rampant in churches. They are the root of so many of the differences in denominations and problems in the Christian faith. They have nothing to do with real Christianity.

FUNCTIONS AND TYPES OF DEMONS

The first step in Satan's strategy for the destruction of a human soul is to identify and focus on a weakness. If the door to that weakness is left open, he may send a particular spirit to enlarge upon it. All spirits have names and specific functions.

For instance, if a person has a tendency toward pride and neither repents nor tries to keep it under control, that sin is a legal entry point for a demonic spirit which is looking for a body. That person then may be saddled with a spirit of pride which he cannot control, other than through conscious binding or deliverance.

Scripture refers to many types of spirits, among which are:

Blind and dumb spirit	(Matt. 12:22)
Unclean spirit	(Mark 1:23)
Deaf and dumb spirit	(Mark 9:25)
Spirit of sickness	(Luke 13:11)
Spirit of divination	(Acts 16:16)
Deceitful spirits	(I Timothy 4:1)
Familiar spirit	(Leviticus 20:27)

Spirit of jealousy	(Numbers 5:14)
Spirit of distortion	(Isaiah 19:14)
Spirit of harlotry	(Hosea 4:12)
Lying spirit	(I Kings 22:23)

Some afflict physically, some mentally, some emotionally and others socially or within the realm of relationships.

Spirits that are mentioned in the Bible are rulers of darkness, but a whole family of related spirits may be present with a ruling spirit. For instance, an unclean spirit will do anything it can to defile a body. It may bring with it spirits of fornication, bestiality, homosexuality, incest, pornography or anything that seeks to defile the body and pervert the soul. In order to uncover the ruling spirit, it is necessary to discover what rules a person.

Many people speak of Jezebel spirits or Delilah spirits or some other Biblical name attached to a spirit. While these designations may be helpful in describing a certain type of spirit, demons usually bear the name of their particular function. For instance, a spirit of rejection will cause a person to feel rejected and to reject others.

When one speaks of a "Delilah spirit", one is not necessarily implying that it is the same spirit that demonized Delilah, but rather that the characteristics of the spirit are like those of the spirit that caused Delilah to destroy Sampson. A "Delilah Spirit" is an extremely destructive influence in a person. It seeks to destroy the person or persons who are the focus of its attention. When it detects any weakness in a person, it capitalizes on the weakness and exaggerates its importance. If it is not dealt with, it will completely destroy the people around it.

It is unclear whether Satan commissions particular

spirits to demonize particular bodies or whether the spirits themselves make the decision where to go. There are instances in Scripture, for instance with King Ahab and the lying spirit, where the Lord put a lying spirit in the mouths of the prophets to entice Ahab into battle against Ramoth Gilead where he was killed. While some have suggested that this was a spirit of God who simply took on the task of enticing Ahab, that explanation does not wash because God does not lie, nor would any spirit of God lie (I Samuel 15:29). God has a plan and He sometimes uses His defeated foe as a pawn in the fulfilment of His plan. In I Corinthians 5:5, Paul instructs the church in Corinth to hand an unrepentant brother over to Satan, *"so that the sinful nature may be destroyed and his spirit saved on the day of the Lord"*.

WORKS OF THE FLESH
Many Christians dismiss any talk of demons saying that whatever problems people have are more results of "works of the flesh" than anything to do with evil spirits. They say that blaming things on Satan is just a way of rationalizing our own failure to discipline ourselves.

Sometimes they're right. In the fifth chapter of Galatians, we're given a list of fifteen of these "works of the flesh":

> sexual immorality
> impurity
> debauchery
> idolatry
> witchcraft
> hatred
> discord
> jealousy
> fits of rage

selfish ambition
dissensions
factions
envy
drunkenness
orgies and the like

Through our experience in the deliverance ministry, we have seen spirits respond to every one of these designations. What then can we say about what is flesh and what is demonic?

When a person is tempted, it can be the first stage of demonization. We have ungodly temptations daily. Since we know that the source of evil is either Satan or our own fallen natures, we know that the source of ungodly temptations is either Satan or our fallen natures. Stimuli are either godly or ungodly - acceptable to God or unacceptable to God. The flesh is the reactor.

When a person yields to an ungodly temptation, he or she sins in the flesh. The reactor then has gone the route of a negative stimulus and the system fails. At this point, the person has the choice of repenting (feeling sorrow for the sin, asking forgiveness of God and determining never to do that thing again), or dallying in the sin, enjoying the pleasure for awhile, perhaps meaning to get right with God later.

What many people either don't realize or choose to reject is the fact that when a person sins, a door is opened for possible demonic entrance. If that door is closed by immediate repentance, there is no cause for concern. However, the longer that door is left open, the greater the possibility that Satan will use it to plant one of his agents.

The problem for the human then becomes two-fold. He or she loses control in the area of the sin. For instance, if the sin was an act of lying, lack of repentance or confession will open the door to lying spirits. (Note that this is in the plural. There are times when a person may be delivered of a spirit and go home wondering why he is still behaving the same way as he/she did before the deliverance. It may be because several spirits of like nature were resident and some stayed hidden while only one or a few left, in which case it is important to reenter the battle.)

The solution is also two-fold: crucify the flesh (deny its demands) and cast out the demons.

Sin in a person's life does not always preclude the entrance of demonic spirits. Sometimes a person can participate in sin or entertain sinful thoughts for a long time with no demonic involvement. Perhaps Satan and his troops simply have not been made aware of the existence of the open door. Satan is not omniscient. He is not all-knowing as God is. His is limited. For instance, a person can fall into lust either as a result of his own fallen nature or as a result of demonic temptation. If it is as a result of his own nature, it may be some time before Satan discovers and takes advantage of the open door. However, who is to know the source of the original thought? No amount of dabbling in sin is safe.

ENTRY POINTS

Demons cannot be 'caught' or 'picked up'. They gain access to a person's life through open doors or opportunities. Scripture warns us against giving place to the devil (Eph. 4:27).

1. The family line:

Exodus 20:5 says, *"I, the Lord your God, am a jealous God, punishing the children for the sin of the fathers to the third and fourth generation of those who hate me"*. Spirits that are passed through the bloodline in families are often the most difficult to detect because they are not viewed as abnormal. A mother may shake her head and sigh, "Well, I guess he has his daddy's temper", as her little darling throws a major temper tantrum right in the middle of the supermarket. Family weaknesses tend to be regarded as things that we 'just have to live with', for instance, "Schizophrenia has been in our family for generations."

The thrilling part about the Exodus 20 passage is that verse five leads to verse six which says, *"but showing love to a thousand generations of those who love Me and keep My commandments"*.!!! Wow! The cycle of infected lives can be broken through the turning of a heart toward Jesus! If anyone who loves Christ is suffering the leftovers of generational sin, he or she can just step out of that thing like one would discard an old pair of jeans and step into freedom with the breaking of the curse through faith in Jesus. Awesome.

2. Childhood:

Satan is no gentleman. He has no sense of fair play. Most of the things we struggle with in our adult lives were planted within us in childhood, sometimes while we were still in the womb. Children are extremely impressionable and vulnerable (Gal.4:1-3).

If a mother resents her pregnancy and does not want the child within, her rejection of the baby can be an open door for a spirit of rejection to fasten itself to that child. Unless the parents or some caring people learn how to pray for that child and do warfare for him or her, he will not only attract rejection from many people throughout life, but he will reject the love of others, thus not learning either to give or receive love freely.

Ephesians 6:4 instructs fathers to *"bring them up in the discipline and instruction of the Lord"*. Through being diligent in training children in the ways of the Lord, parents can lead children on safe paths that will keep them from all kinds of difficulties. When parents fail to be consistent and goal oriented in the area of Christian training, the children lose through parental default.

If a parent threatens to leave a spouse over and over again, the child will feel very insecure, thus leaving an open door to spirits of fear, insecurity, apprehension, dread, worry and others of like nature.

If a parent is constantly criticizing people in front of a child, the child may believe that this is an acceptable form of behaviour and open the door to a spirit of accusation and any of its associates.

When children experience abuse in the formative years, they almost invariably experience demonic interference in their lives. Abuse can happen in any one of four areas; physical, sexual, emotional and spiritual.

Spiritual abuse takes place when a child is involuntarily placed in the position of receiving demonic or occult powers that are either passed down through the family line, transmitted through occult rituals or imposed on the child in the form of a curse.

3. Occult influence:

Any assenting involvement with occult paraphernalia such as Ouija boards, Dungeon and Dragon games, yoga meditation, fortune telling, astrology, horoscopes, tarot cards, crystals, etc., are like ushers at open doors, saying, "Come on in!". Wilful, persistent sin invites demonic habitation.

Many Christians hang on to superstitions or irrational fears. Occult traditions have been passed down through the centuries and have become integral aspects of our culture.

We do not have to go to the jungles of Africa to find witchcraft in action. It has become an increasingly visible part of suburban life. So called white witches perform everything from simple rituals to heavy duty spells and incantations over people supposedly for their benefit. We have had people come to us who are involved in voodoo practices right here in Toronto and are linked through the spirit realm to people in other countries.

We have people who swear that they actually see people who they know who live thousands of miles away via astro travel.

I had a visit one day from a woman who was so frightened that she was almost jumping out of her skin. She proceeded to tell me that she had fled to Canada with her eight year old daughter from a husband who was terribly violent and who, along with his family, was deeply involved in the occult. He had promised that she would pay for her actions and recently she had been experiencing strange things in her home. Things were moving around mysteriously and she was filled with an overwhelming sense of dread. That day, while her daughter was with her in the kitchen, the little girl had exclaimed, "Mommy! Daddy is here! I see him. He is over there!". As the woman looked towards the direction in which the child was pointing, she saw a dark shadow moving although she was unable to distinguish characteristics. What a relief it was to her as we drove out the spirits that had accompanied her husband's curse on the family.

Over and over again we have see horrible examples of charlatans who seem to have no conscience at all about taking advantage of people who are blinded by superstition.

One man who believed himself to be a Christian, but

who also practised witchcraft, came to us requesting that we remove a curse on his family. He was bankrupt from paying a 'godfather' thousands of dollars to remove this curse and finally ended up at our doorstep, having heard that we did not charge for 'these services'. Apparently his family had experienced some mysterious illnesses and this 'godfather' had interpreted these as a curse that had been placed on the family by some people who were envious of them. He tricked them into believing him and then told them that in order to remove the curse, they had to perform a ritual stronger than their enemy's ritual. When the 'godfather's' first fee of $4,000.00 did not provide relief, another fee was required for another attempt at performing a stronger ritual than that of the enemy. When over $100,000.00 had been spent with no success, the well was finally dry and the 'godfather' was suddenly no longer interested in trying to help. Happily, that man and his family found Jesus and are now on their way to Heaven.

Many Christians practice their Christianity more out of superstition than out of love for Jesus. How about the parents who bring their babies for dedication to have the children 'done'? They think it will bring some sort of good luck to the children, with no understanding of the commitment in dedicating themselves to raising the children in the love and teachings of Christ. While this may not constitute an entry point for demonic involvement, it surely is a response to a deception of the enemy.

4. Unforgiveness:

Matthew 18:33-35 tells the conclusion of Jesus' story about the unmerciful servant who was forgiven a great debt by his master but refused to forgive someone who owed him. When onlookers witnessed the injus-

132

tice, they went to the unmerciful servant's master who called him in and said, *"You wicked servant. I cancelled all of that debt of yours because you begged me to. Shouldn't you have mercy on your fellow servant just as I had on you?"*

Jesus finished the story with this warning: *"In anger, his masters turned him over to the jailers to be tortured, until he should pay back all he owed. This is how My Heavenly Father will treat each of you unless you forgive your brother from your heart."*

When we don't forgive, tormenting spirits can be released into our lives. They will destroy us, causing chemical changes in our bodies which produce all manner of diseases.

In "None of these Diseases", Dr. S.I. McMillen's classic work on how Scripture predates modern medicine, Dr. McMillen details the process whereby the emotional centre of the brain produces widespread physical changes by means of three principal mechanisms: by changing the amount of blood flowing to an organ, by affecting the secretions of various glands, and by changing the tension of muscles.

Tormenting spirits focus their energies on disrupting the emotional centre of the brain.

When Jesus said in Matt. 18:22 that we are to forgive seventy times seven times, he knew that it wasn't just for the good of our souls, but also for the preservation of our bodies, for prevention of things like ulcerative colitis, toxic goitres, high blood pressure, strokes, bleeding ulcers, kidney disease etc.

Dr. McMillen tells of the results of a study at one hospital that showed that resentment was the most prominent personality characteristic of the victims of mucous colitis, occurring in ninety-six percent of the participants of the study.

5. Lack of self-discipline:

God takes care of our spirits. He seals us. However, we are responsible for our souls and bodies. 2 Cor. 10:4,5 talks about taking every thought captive and bringing it into obedience to Christ. If we don't 'crucify the flesh' or sacrifice the demands of our bodies in favour of Scriptural principles, we leave wide open doors for demonic interference in our lives.

At first, Saul was simply jealous of David, but as he entertained his jealous thoughts, a spirit of jealousy walked right in and settled down.

A person who doesn't deal with his or her anxieties but stuffs them with food will invite spirits of bondage to take over in the area of eating. Soon, thoughts of food will torment the victim in every waking hour, promising relief with indulgence but paying up with a bloated body and a mind filled with self loathing.

6. Transference of spirits:

I Kings 16-22 details the story of King Ahab and Jezebel. Ahab was a good king until he allowed Jezebel to infect his life with her evil ways. If a person sleeps with dogs, chances are he or she will get fleas. If we come into agreement in our hearts with people who are demonized, we build bridges from our lives to theirs, over which the spirits which infect their lives are permitted to travel, toll free.

Some people fear praying for a demonized person for fear the spirits will come out of the one being prayed for and enter the one praying. That has happened, but only when the person praying is not under the protection of the blood of Jesus, having left open doors in his own life through one means or another. Remember the seven sons of Sceva in Acts 19:14. They were attempting to drive out demons without themselves having a personal relationship with Jesus, but simply invoking His name as a form of ritual in the deliverance. One day when they were doing this, an evil spirit called them on their credentials and attacked them ferociously, sending them running from the house naked and bleeding. It must have been quite a sight.

It is extremely important, however, for this story to be taken within the context of its intent. Believers in Jesus are to be fearless in commanding spirits to leave demonized people. They have full authority to do so in the Name of Jesus. The purpose of this story is to warn unspiritual people of the dangers involved in tampering with the spiritual realm. Deliverance is no game.

THIS IS WITH JESUS SAID 'DON'T LET YOUR HEART TO BE TROUBLED

7. Circumstances:

Emotional crises can be prime opportunities for demonic entrance. Even when sin may not be a factor, if a person becomes totally overwhelmed by the circumstances of the moment, he or she may become trapped in bondage through not knowing how to handle distress.

We have a friend who was driving her children home one icy cold winter night. As she rounded the curve of a cloverleaf onto a highway, her car hit some black ice and became airborne as the wheels hit the cement curb and sent the car hurtling totally out of control towards the highway. At the instant of trauma, our friend yelled, "Jesus", putting control of her children, her life and her car immediately into the Lord's hands. Unseen hands took that car which by now was facing in the opposite direction and set it down on the shoulder of the road, out of danger from the oncoming traffic. What could have been a frightening trauma was turned into a thrilling memory of angelic ministry for our friend and her children. All the way home they talked excitedly about what God had done in the circumstance.

We have another young friend who, in similar circumstances, did not call out to Jesus but felt herself knocked into stultifying fear. She has since refused to drive on any highways and is in bondage to fear of driving, fear of failure, discouragement and inadequacy. She was not mature enough in her relationship with Jesus to be able to abandon herself into His arms in a time of trouble. She is, however, growing in the Lord and will one day be free of the fears that bind her. People who nearly drown can be overcome by a fear of water. People who are bitten by dogs can develop an unnatural fear of dogs. Any trauma can be an open door for demonic interference. It is very important to pray following any fearful occurrence and make sure that there are no unwanted spiritual residues.

Abuse at any stage of life can be an entry point for unholy spirits. For instance, if a spouse suffers psychological abuse through emotional abandonment, it opens the door to all kinds of spirits of depression, discouragement, loneliness etc.

8. Cursed items:

Deuteronomy 7:25,26 warns against the spiritual ramifications of possessing cursed items. *"The images of their gods you are to burn in the fire. Do not covet the silver and gold on them, and do not take it for yourselves, or you will be ensnared by it, for it is detestable to the Lord your God. Do not bring a detestable thing into your house or you, like it, will be set apart for destruction."*

Often, when people travel to Africa or Mexico or other lands where idols are commonplace, they buy interesting artifacts as decorations for their homes, not realizing that some of these things may have been used by witch doctors in heathen worship or what-ever. Demons can definitely be attracted to homes through artifacts and books pertaining to idols, the occult and all kinds of false religions.

We have a friend who, on hearing about the potential for evil influence in some of these things, went through her house and collected a whole pile of things that might possibly be problematic. She put everything in a big plastic bag, took it out to her garage and smashed it all with a sledgehammer. When questioned about the necessity of including some of the things she destroyed, she responded that if there was even a teeny chance of anything having an adverse affect on her family, she didn't want it.

There is certainly merit to that approach. However, it is probably better to ask God for direction if any items are the root of spiritual distress. Otherwise, things can be sacrificed unnecessarily.

9. Ignorance:

Perhaps the most common way that demons gain access to a host body is through ignorance of the human. Because we usually can't see into the spirit realm with our natural eyes, most people act as though it doesn't exist.

For instance, sometimes we say things like, "You don't love me", to a spouse, not really meaning that we believe that, but simply to get reassurance that he or she does love us. The problem is that through that negative confession, we open the door for demonic interference. Rather than receiving the reassurance we solicited, we have given an opening for any number of things to come upon us - rejection, resentment, exasperation, abandonment ad infinitum.

The words we speak with our mouths are of far greater importance than we can imagine.

It is no small wonder that the secular world regards much of Christendom with disdain. We are like a besieged city that opened its gates to its enemies and sat watching while they plundered, killed and destroyed.

CHAPTER NINE

RESTORING THE SOUL

This world is full of souls in pain. Where does one go for relief?

Deliverance is not always the answer. Even when it is, we have found that aching souls are often safe havens for demon spirits and there needs to be a measure of soul restoration before deliverance can be truly effective.

So - where does one go to restore the soul?

Soul stores where old souls can be traded in on fresh new ones are a fanciful thought. How about soul bypasses or transplants?

Uh-uh. Each person gets only one soul and has to deal with it.

The problem is that by the time we admit that we really are in trouble, our souls are often in such shambles that the very idea of fixing them is totally beyond us. Even if we do know what to do, we have usually been so weakened by that point that we don't have the strength to 'deal with it' on our own.

SOUL DOCTORS

So how about soul doctors, people who help us to restore our souls?

Psychiatrists go to school for many years to learn how to restore souls. They are paid big dollars for their services. However, I have yet to meet a soul restored by a psychiatrist. Of course many people have been helped through difficult times and have been guided in their understanding of why things are as they are in their lives, but I've yet to meet a psychiatrist who has actually restored one soul. There are those who have actually increased rather than decreased a client's problems. Just as in anything else, there are gifted psychiatrists but there are also charlatans.

Churches claim to be place where souls can get cleaned up and polished. The problem is that once people get involved in churches they often find them to be support groups for tarnished souls in distress rather than hospitals for healing.

Webster's New World Dictionary defines "restore" as, *"to make strong, to give back (something taken away, lost etc.); make restitution of; to bring back to a former or normal condition, as by repairing, rebuilding, altering, etc.; to put (a person) back in place, position, rank etc.; to bring back to health, strength, etc.; to reestablish something which has passed away".*

Where then, is this soul restoration to be found?

Scripture says, *"He (the Lord) restores my soul"* (Psalm 23:3).

Are there any words on earth more reassuring? *"He restores my soul".*

Not 'He might be able to restore my soul', or 'He's going to restore a piece of my soul', or 'He's restoring my friend's soul', but *"He restores my soul"*, my whole soul.

SOUL RESTORATION ISN'T...

Some have called this the "healing of memories" or "inner healing". Certain teachers, even some who are very high profile have gotten off track in this area to the extent that many Christians shudder at the very mention of these phrases. Unfortunately, some ministries have allowed occult inroads with use of such methods as visualization and endless cycles of churning up every little scrap of injustice like hamsters on wheels. It's as though they've forgotten the work of the cross.

Soul restoration has nothing to do with conscious manipulation of memories through visualization of changes. It is not creative imagination. It has nothing to do with Psychology. Neither does it have anything to do with forcing people to dredge up painful areas of their lives without the leading of the Lord. Although the phrase sounds comforting, soul restoration is not just a cultic comfort zone. It is much, much more than that.

SOUL RESTORATION IS...

Soul restoration refers to the process by which Christ makes people *aware* of areas in their lives that need to be redeemed and then takes them through the stages of *repentance, forgiveness and settlement*. It is a supernatural process administered, supervised and nurtured by the Lord Jesus Christ.

Awareness - Jesus knows which areas of our lives hold us back in relationship with Him. Certain responses to specific circumstances which have formed negative attitudes in our hearts can be fertile soil for demonic maintenance. Being made aware of the troublesome areas is the first step towards restoration of the soul.

Repentance - Having a change of heart, feeling a deep sorrow for ungodly attitudes or actions and deciding to make a change, no matter what the cost is the second stage of soul restoration. Galatians 6:7 says, *"Do not be deceived, God is not mocked; for whatever a man sows, that shall he also reap"*. There are no exceptions. Reaping what one sows is an eternal, unchanging, immutable law of God. God loves His children. Scripture says that He looks on them with compassion (Psalm 103:13). He doesn't want them to sow destruction unto themselves. As He pricks the heart about a certain memory, attitude, response or plan, He invites the soul to repentance, which will free it from reaping eternal destruction.

Repentance does not just mean crying buckets of tears at some altar with the organ playing dolorous strains of "Just as I Am". It means a deep, sincere recognition of the pain that we have caused the Lord and a willingness to allow Him to change us no matter how difficult the change may be nor what accustomed pleasures we may lose in the process.

It is not enough to be sorry or forgiven. Repentance involves nailing our destructive habits, attitudes or responses to the cross and leaving them there, where they are no longer part of us.

Forgiveness - The next step in soul restoration is prayer requesting forgiveness from God. It may also involve laying down our attitudes towards others and forgiving them for whatever we hold in our hearts toward them.

Sometimes the most difficult aspect of forgiveness is forgiveness of the self. People often feel so guilty about what has happened that they feel that they don't deserve forgiveness. They need to recognize the fact that God promises to forgive those who confess their sins and if God has forgiven them then they have no right to withhold forgiveness from themselves.

There are those who will counsel people to forgive God if they have held Him responsible for some pain in their lives. However, God never needs forgiveness because God never does anything faintly sinful. He does everything perfectly. Just because we may not understand doesn't mean that God's plan for our lives in wrong. People who hold bitterness against Him need to be loved into a recognition of their wrongful attitudes and ask God to forgive them for their bitterness against Him.

142

Settlement - The final stage of restoration of the soul is a 'no doubt about it' change of heart, acceptance of forgiveness and a determination to be persistent until everything about the situation has been laid to rest. Whenever any of the old bitter feelings begin to surface they must be immediately put under the blood. Whenever any temptation to come into agreement with any temptation raises its head it must be nailed to the cross and left there.

When Jesus completed His work on the cross, He said, *"It is finished"* (John 19:30). When He completes the stages of soul restoration in our hearts, the work in that area is finished. It has been settled and we must let it go.

Settlement is a process of continuously reminding oneself and Satan that the work has been completed until it is no longer even a ripple of concern.

SEEKING REFUGE FOR THE SOUL

Often when people come to us, their souls are in pieces. They are in great emotional distress as a result of the past or present circumstances of their lives.

We discovered through the process of learning how to minister deliverance that there are times when little progress can be made in freeing people from darkness until there has been a measure of restoration of the soul.

As people's souls are gently restored, Jesus strengthens them in their 'inner man' so that they can better stand against Satan.

SOUL RESTORATION IS OFTEN PRELIMINARY TO *EFFECTIVE* DELIVERANCE

In order for people to be set free, it is helpful for them to be consciously aware of the things that bind them and be able to focus on release from those things. People are often vaguely aware of things being out of kilter but they may have been unable to put their finger on the root of the problem.

Once certain aspects of their lives are seen through a Godly perspective and once people put themselves in line with God's Word in terms of their responses, Satan then has no more legal ground to remain and the demons are easily routed.

It is true that evil spirits can be cast out without any ministry to the soul, because they do have to flee when commanded to do so by the authority of the Name of Jesus. However, if there has been no restoration of the soul before the demons have been displaced, they may still have legal ground to stay in the person's life and simply return when all of the fuss is over.

For instance, a man harbouring bitterness toward an uncle who molested him as a child, may have had a bitter spirit enter through the open door years before which resides there legally in the man's attitude of unforgiveness. In that case, even when the Name of Jesus is spoken, it may be like pulling hens' teeth to get the spirit out. When forgiveness is accomplished, however, it has no more legal ground to stand on and flushes out much more easily.

EMILY

Normally, whenever people come to us for deliverance, we like to make an appointment to get to know them to assess the situation before jumping right into deliverance. This usually leads to a few counselling sessions where we ask the Lord to illumine areas that need to be healed and encourage the people to tell us about themselves, suggesting that they take us on a brief walk through their childhoods. Invariably, situations of disharmony between parents and children, or instances of deviation from God's laws which have resulted in the reaping of difficult circumstances, come to light. We take these things to Jesus together and He leads them through soul restoration or healing of their memories and eventually into deliverance.

When Emily's parents brought her to see us, they claimed that their daughter, a lovely young woman who had just graduated from a Christian college, was demonized. As proof, they cited her inability to pray and her violent epileptic seizures.

Because they had travelled a considerable distance and were limited for time, we bypassed the usual assessment stage. They appeared to be Christian people of discernment and concern for their daughter and so we proceeded towards setting Emily free.

Whenever we approach deliverance, we always test the spirits by commanding them to manifest their presence in some way. If there is no manifestation, we know that we are not dealing with a spirit but with a natural characteristic of the person.

This time, there was no question. Emily immediately began to act like a three year old child - a very unappealing three year old. She threw her Kleenex at her parents, whined, "I don't wanna be here!" and kicked and screamed her way into a very undignified temper tantrum.

Suddenly she was once more a mature young graduate - and just as suddenly a rebellious toddler again. We realized that we were dealing with a split personality and stopped the deliverance to find out when and why Emily's personality had fragmented.

As we talked, the real story came pouring forth.

When Emily was just a little girl, her parents had been having severe marriage problems which resulted in intense frustrations. The mother had begun to abuse

Emily emotionally and physically. One day, in total exasperation, she grabbed the little girl and flung her against the wall, hitting her head so hard that the child began to have seizures.

Alternating between periods of rage and overwhelming guilt, the mother began to spoil Emily, giving her whatever she wanted following her rages.

In a situation such as this, the child generally accepts the mother's behaviour as normal and blanks out the pain and fear in exchange for the rewards, whether emotional or material, that follow the rage.

As the parents openly poured out their guilt ridden story with deep sobs and anguish over the physical and emotional pain they had inflicted on their daughter, Emily began to understand things. The angry child was finally able to forgive her parents and Emily was able to put the little girl to rest, accepting the responsibility of being an adult.

Because there was no further legal ground for Satan, the spirits were easily routed.

FANTASY OF VIOLENCE

It is obvious from reading the daily newspapers that fantasies of violence are far from uncommon. It is also not uncommon for Christians to conclude that these fantasies are demonically rooted.

That may be so in many cases, but not always.

I personally struggled for many years with a a most troubling fantasy. While I loved women in general and felt particularly protective towards any woman who was pregnant, I had a totally out-of-character, perverse desire to kick or punch pregnant women right in the stomach.

I am not a violent man. I have never been a violent man. When my wife was expecting our children I thought that she was the most beautiful creature in the entire universe, and yet this crazy fantasy dogged my imagination. It really made me wonder what kind of a man I actually was.

I tried to think back over my life to figure out where this bizarre thing originated, but nothing made any sense.

I was born during the great Depression as the fifth child to a mother who was close to forty years of age. My parents loved me so much that I should have been the envy of all of my siblings, and yet they all loved me too. I was a well balanced, healthy individual from a strong Italian family. Why, then, did I carry a deep sense of rejection and a lonely feeling of not fitting in?

One might have concluded that I was simply demonized and needed to be delivered of the thing that plagued me. Nothing else seemed to make any sense. During a time of prayer when others were praying over me for soul restoration, the Lord made me aware of the source of my dysfunction and led me through to the place of release.

As the group prayed, I felt as though I was confined inside a close fitting, cast iron cage. Despite the strength of the walls, they were soft and coloured a deep blood red. I was terribly uncomfortable and felt a deep sense of being imprisoned in the wrong place. In my discomfort I was aware of the leader of the group asking the Lord to forgive my parents if they had felt any sense of rejection toward me or if they had considered an abortion while I was in the womb. As he continued to pray, he encouraged me to forgive my parents for anything negative that happened to me before I was born.

I did that, despite my lack of any solid understanding of events or feelings during that time. As I voiced my forgiveness, I felt an actual release from that cage and 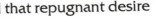 I have never since experienced that repugnant desire to inflict injury on an expectant mother.

What was the whole story? I don't know. I never did ask my mother for details of those days. I suppose that, considering the danger of war, the shortage of food, the already large family and the age of my parents, I was probably a mistake - an unplanned pregnancy. I doubt that my mother would ever have considered an actual abortion, but who knows? Perhaps she was depressed and wished that she would miscarry so that she and my father would not be responsible for feeding another mouth.

Whatever the 'then', the 'now' is that I have wonderful memories of being dearly loved as a child and I have been set free of my troubles. Why should it be necessary to dig up and expose all of the pain of the past, embarrass my Mom and allow bad memories to displace all of the warmth of my childhood?

Once the Lord pinpointed the area in my life that needed to be redeemed and I went through the stages of repentance for my thoughts, forgiving my parents and solidly concluding that I was free, Satan had no grounds for troubling me in that area and simply vacated it.

THE PROCESS OF RESTORATION

The restoration of the soul is a process Christ uses to mature His people, to strengthen them and to set them free from things in their pasts which cripple them.

It often involves prayer and counsel from other Christians who understand what it means to love their brothers and sisters into greater freedom in Christ.

When Jesus raised Lazarus from the dead, Lazarus was a new man, just as we are when we find new life in Christ. However, new or not, when Lazarus was raised, the general consensus was that, *"he stinketh"*!

(John 11:39). He was wrapped from head to toe in grave clothes that bound him from living any kind of free, fulfilling life until they could be removed. Jesus instructed those around him to remove the grave clothes, just as He instructs us today to help our brothers and sisters out of the habits and attitudes which keep them bound.

CHAPTER TEN

DELIVERANCE

Matt came with a friend one Friday evening in the early days of our ministry group. He appeared to be a rather quiet, shy man with a gentle nature. He claimed to love the Lord and shared some seemingly sincere testimony of how he had experienced God's faithfulness in His life that very day.

I didn't think about him again until two weeks later when he showed up once again at our meeting, this time with a few more apparently Christian friends.

As the meeting began and we entered into a time of praise and worship, I felt impressed to spend more time in earnest prayer. I really felt the need of the protection of the Holy Spirit. I knew that something unusual was going to happen that evening. I told the group what the Holy Spirit had shown me, and so rather than spend the usual amount of time in singing, we began to pray and spent some time in silence listening for direction from God.

A word of knowledge came to me concerning a person who was so discouraged that he was at the end of his rope and was considering ending his life. I spoke the word forth and asked whoever the person was to come up for prayer.

With no hesitancy, Matt stood and made his way to the front of the group. There he fell to his knees and began to sob deep, soul wrenching sobs. A couple of his friends came forward to comfort him. I asked one of them what was wrong with Matt, and he said that his friend had been talking about wanting to die.

I sat down on the floor comfortably in front of Matt and began to comfort him, asking him why he was so discouraged.

151

Between deep sobs and anguished wails, he told me that he had nothing to live for and simply wanted to be with Jesus.

Assuming that Matt really was the gentle, kind man that he had portrayed, I made myself more comfortable and began to minister to him. Just as I began to command the spirit of death to leave him, Matt looked up at me and smiled the weirdest smile.

Just for a second, I took my eyes off of him and suddenly his fist came out of nowhere and connected like a cement truck with my jaw!

As an ex-Iranian soldier in the group and some others pinned Matt to the floor, I scrambled to my feet in shock. Matt jerked and twisted as he growled like a fierce dog in his attempts to get at me.

I was stunned, but I knew that the enemy had to submit to the Spirit of God and so I bound the spirits in the Name of Jesus and told the men to let go of Matt because we had power over whatever was within him.

As they released him I told Matt to fight the demons within himself and command them to go, but He was too weak.

As the others prayed and sang about the Name of Jesus and His blood, I took authority once again and the spirit of death left.

Matt looked up, very weak and shaken by the ordeal, but with a wonderful expression of peace on his face. I made an appointment to see him early the following week.

That night, as I assessed the damage to my face, it bothered me greatly that Matt had been able to attack me. Thoughts of the seven sons of Sceva troubled me and I wondered what I had done wrong.

I knew that I should have had full authority over Satan. I asked God to show me the answers.

When Matt and I met the following week, he poured out his story to me. As it turned out, the kind, gentle mask was simply a paper thin cover for the rage filled inner man. He had been a child of abuse who graduated his teens as an alcoholic drug junkie, charged at least once with sexual assault. His mind had been so fried by drugs that he had been regarded as a vegetable. An absolute reject of society, Matt's lack of self esteem often led him to release his frustrations with violence against whatever or whoever was closest.

As we discussed the punch, Matt said that just before he hit me, he had heard a crazy laughter in his head and the humiliation of feeling laughed at by the spirit of rage within him made him lash out at the closest thing - my face.

Now I understood. It was not the demon who had attacked me. It was a wounded man who's habitual response to rejection was violence.

We proceeded to expel the spirit of rage which was a hindrance to Matt's growth and step by step, Matt's soul was restored as he experienced the healing of his memories and further deliverance. Happily, he has learned to be in control of his life and is able to be a great help to those around him.

We learned a great deal from our experience with Matt.

Those in ministry can never afford to accept anything according to surface appearances. One must always look to the Lord for discernment. It is imperative to be alert at every moment (Eph.6:18). I will never again relax while praying for someone. When the Holy Spirit warns of danger, we need to be on full alert and pray in the Spirit. Since that time, we almost invariably spend preliminary time with people before entering into any kind of deliverance with them.

WHY CAST OUT DEMONS?

If polled, probably eighty percent of Christians would opt for no involvement with demonology. They are afraid of stirring up something that they have no idea how to handle. They think that if they keep their heads stuck in the sand, all of the nasty things in life will simply go away.

Had Matt taken that approach, he probably would have been either in jail or dead by now. As it is, he is leading a strong, productive life, the life that Christ died to give him.

"Yes, but his was an extreme case", some may say.

That's true, but he *looked* great on the outside - as do most Christians. Inside, many of them are blocked from leading the abundant lives that Christ promised because of Satan's interference.

Matt was not an exception. We meet and deal with many Matts.

The pathetic Christians are the ones who make valiant efforts to hobble along spiritually, never confronting and routing the forces that cripple them.

Christ came to establish His Kingdom, to redeem mankind from Satan. Deliverance from demonization is all part of what He came to do.

Because of what Christ accomplished on the cross, we have a right to reclaim territory that Satan has taken. We have a right to face him and demand that he set our spouses and children free. I Corinthians 7:14 says that, *"The unbelieving husband has been sanctified (set apart for God's purposes) through his wife, and the unbelieving wife has been sanctified through her believing husband. Otherwise your children would be unclean, but as it is, they are holy".*

We need to get angry about the devastation Satan has caused in our lives, recognize that as a defeated foe he has no right to continue, take back the ground that

154

he has stolen and stand firmly against him so that he can take no more.

If we could see with our natural eyes the ugly, misshapen things that we allow to fasten themselves to our lives, we would be stunned. The fact that we apathetically carry them around for years and put up with the pain they inflict upon us needlessly is too ridiculous for words. That we would allow these filthy creatures to break up our marriages, keep us in poverty, keep us smoking cancer sticks or all of the other dysfunctions they inflict upon us is truly amazing.

ONE MORE NIGHT WITH THE FROGS?

When Pharaoh was hit with the plague of frogs, he told Moses to deliver Egypt of the frogs the next day. Why did he procrastinate? He could have been rid of those slimy things instantly. By putting it off, he no doubt had frogs in his soup for dinner, frogs in his pyjamas when he got dressed for bed, frogs squishing under his slippered feet as he walked the palace halls, frogs in his bed and frogs in his shaving mug the next morning. Why? Because he was not a man of action. He knew the frogs were there, but he was a waffler and had to think about things for awhile.

Thinking didn't get rid of the frogs anymore than thinking about getting rid of demonic interference in our lives routs the evil spirits.

Jesus dedicated about thirty percent of His ministry to teaching about spiritual warfare and delivering people from evil spirits. He warned us repeatedly about preparing ourselves for eternity rather than dwelling on earthly affairs. If deliverance does not have any eternal significance in our lives, why was it so important to Jesus?

PURIFICATION - ESTHER STYLE

When Esther prepared herself to meet the King, she spent a whole year in intense purification processes. Esther 2:12 tells us that she spent the first six months in applications of oil of myrrh and the following six months being treated with special perfumes and cosmetics. Everything was provided by the King but it was Esther who had to submit herself to the purification and preparation process.

The oil speaks to us of our need to be anointed with the oil of the Holy Spirit and the perfumes and spices are symbolic of the fruit and gifts of the Spirit.

This story underlines the importance of preparing ourselves to meet our King. Esther couldn't run haphazardly into her King's presence, expecting to become magically perfect at the instant of their meeting. How much more do we as the Bride of Christ need to be purified and cleansed from all evil.

Satan does everything he can to keep us from having strong Christian personalities ripe with the fruit of the Spirit, operating in power through His gifts.

For instance, one of the fruits of the Spirit is love. If a Christian begins to foster resentment towards someone and allows the resentment to grow into hatred, a spirit of hatred may take up residence and make it impossible for the Christian to give off a lovely aroma of God's love. Complicating matters may be a whole family of related spirits such as bitterness and jealousy that may enter with hatred.

If we allow Satan to continue his attack on our lives whether through our emotions, our finances, our relationships or whatever he may be doing, we allow him to weaken our Christian witness. On the contrary, when people see us living strong, productive lives, overcoming obstacles with rock solid faith, they "want some of that!", and ground is gained for Christ.

It is impossible to live a genuine Christian life with demonic tag alongs. Warfare must be fought.

HOW TO RECOGNIZE DEMONIC PRESENCE

1. Discernment: I Corinthians 12:10 tells us that the seventh gift of the Spirit for use in the church is the gift of distinguishing between spirits, or discernment of spirits. This is a supernatural ability to recognize demonic presence.

One Friday evening, a woman named Sharon showed up at our ministry group. She had been invited by a friend from her Alcoholics Anonymous group. Sharon was about fifty years old and appeared to be in very poor health. She was of average height but weighed about two hundred and forty pounds. During the meeting, she sat as if frozen in place. When the call was made for those who wanted prayer to come forward, I could see Sharon struggling with the decision of whether or not to come. Finally, she came but when I approached her to pray, she let out a scream and fell on the floor.

When some of the members of the group went to her assistance she jerked violently away from them. As I calmed the people and spoke gently to Sharon, I looked into her eyes. Of course I knew that I was dealing with a demonic spirit. I had seen those eyes many times before. Even without looking at the eyes, however, the Spirit within me flashed a red light warning from the moment Sharon walked into the room.

Because it has become our policy to try not to deal with deliverance in our meetings, we made an appointment to meet with Sharon the following Wednesday night.

157

2. Perception: There is a certain element of detective work involved in deliverance. In our preliminary appointments with people who request deliverance, we try to get as clear a picture as possible of the critical times in their lives where there may have been entry points for demons.

We try to assess their attitudes towards various people and things so that we can see where the trouble spots may be. People say things like, "I feel so confused". At that point we may test the spirit, addressing the 'spirit of confusion'. If it responds, saying something like, "I am not here", we know that it is.

Before Sharon's appointment on Wednesday, we prayed for the Lord's protection and wisdom. At that time, we bound any spirits in Sharon that were not of God and commanded them not to interfere in her release.

When Sharon arrived, we could see that she was very fearful. She was shaking and avoided touching us in any way. She seemed to be very confused.

As we chatted, she revealed that she had lived in fear of almost everything all of her life. She was a slave to drugs and could not pass a drug counter without buying weight loss pills or anything that would speed her up or slow her down. She took them in as large doses as she could.

Besides the drug addiction, she was an alcoholic and addicted to food. She had been to every diet organization imaginable and had found little help although she was finding a measure of relief from her alcoholism at A.A. In desperation, she was going to weekly visits with a psychiatrist who attributed all of her problems to her mind. Of course the real enemy remained undetected and the victim remained a victim.

It quickly became obvious that we were dealing with

several personalities. They began to engage us in a conversation as though there were many people present. At times they spoke in the third person, referring to Sharon as "she" or "Sharon". One personality with a very manly voice and attitude claimed to be Sharon's "protector", claiming that she was very little and suffered a lot.

When we attempted to speak to Sharon, a very confused personality spoke, claiming that it didn't know what to do.

Not until we called on Jesus for help could the real Sharon come forward. We asked her to share what was happening. Hesitantly, she told us that she knew that she had not been the one speaking, She felt as though she was split into pieces and part of her was missing.

When we told her that we believed her, she appeared to be very relieved because she claimed that others hadn't seemed to be able to understand what was happening with her.

We encouraged her by assuring her that we had seen this before with many people and that the Lord Jesus would set her free. Encouraged, Sharon told us about her life and the horrible abuse she had experienced in her childhood.

From time to time as we talked, different personalities emerged and attempted to dominate. Protector was very vocal, insisting that we had no business with Sharon and that he would not let her go. Whenever this happened, we continued to bind the evil spirits, put them under the Blood of Jesus and remind them of their obligation to submit to the Word of God.

Psychiatrists would quite probably have seen this as a case of MPD or Multiple Personality Disorder, meaning that Sharon's personality had segmented. They would have worked perhaps for years trying to integrate all of the personalities into one Sharon.

In actual fact, the personalities resided within Sharon but they certainly were not Sharon.

When we had a reasonably clear picture of what we were dealing with, we began to command the spirits to name themselves and commanded them to come out.

At that point, all Hell broke loose. Although the spirits were bound and could not touch us, they began to struggle intensely, twisting and shaking, screaming and refusing to budge. Sharon's eyes burned a hot fiery red. Her body stiffened and she collapsed on the chair as though dead.

After a few moments, she began to talk, apologising for her behaviour and trying to explain to us that she was not the one who was doing this. She complained of a terrible headache and a very tight band around her head. She claimed to hear a lot of confusion in her head and asked what was going on.

When we explained to her about the spirits that were being stubborn about coming out, she nodded her head, saying that she had suspected their presence for a long time.

As we shared some Scriptures with her, Sharon did not seem to understand at all. Contrary to our original understanding, she now claimed not to be a Christian and to have no real knowledge of what the Bible had to say.

We encouraged her to make a profession of faith, but she could not do it. As we read promises from the Scriptures to her, the screaming began again. "We will not let her go. She is our child. We will fight for her."

As we told Sharon that Jesus loved her, the demon replied, "No, He doesn't. Where was He when she needed Him?".

We commanded the demon to step aside because we

wanted to talk to Sharon. When she was in control of herself, we warned her that she had to make a decision, and if she did not choose Christ, there was no hope for her, because even if we forced the owner of the property out, it would simply return with more spirits and she would be worse off than she was in the beginning.

Sharon agreed. She tried to commit her life to Jesus, but the demons took over and she was unable to speak.

However, it did them no good. For that split second in time, Jesus had seen Sharon's heart and her desire to give her life to Him. Now the demons had no legal ground and had to go.

As we commanded them out, they cried out to their god to help them but of course he couldn't. We quoted Colossians 2:10,15: *"For in Christ all the fullness of the Deity lives in bodily form, and you have been given fullness in Christ who is the head over every power and authority. And having disarmed the powers and authorities, He made a public spectacle of them, triumphing over them by the cross."*.

"No, no", they cried out, "Not that"! Once again we reminded them in the Name of the Father, the Son and the Holy Spirit that they had to go. With a final scream, they left.

It seemed that every fibre of Sharon's being relaxed. She looked at us out of soft, gentle, tear trickling eyes with a smile of joyful contentment on her face. She knew that she was free.

We shared for a little while longer, praying and thanking God for His mercy and power. As we instructed Sharon on how to live in victory without losing the freedom she had gained, she responded as though a whole new world had opened up to her. And it had.

161

By the time she was ready to leave, her entire deportment had changed.

From a frightened, hopeless mess, unable to even touch anyone, she left our office a smiling, vivacious woman praising God. On the way out she gave us the biggest bear hugs we had had in a long time!

Once again, as Carmen and I drove home, we marvelled at the fact that simple people have the power through Jesus to subdue and drive out demons. They had no choice but to obey us. In spite of the fact that just one demon could have overpowered us had we not been protected by the blood of Jesus, we had had no fear or worry, knowing that our God was truly able and that His promises are indeed true.

This was another real faith building experience for us. With this demonstration of God's victory over evil, we were encouraged with the realization once again that God is present in all of the perils of life and He really will supply all of our need.

As we ministered to Sharon throughout the deliverance process, perception of the realities of demonic presence was an important element in our ability to deal with them on a faith basis. We had to believe that they were present in order to believe that they had to go.

COMMON SYMPTOMS OF DEMONIZATION

When Jesus was on earth in the flesh, people recognized the existence of demons. Even non believers came to Him asking Him to get rid of them (Mark 7:24-30). When missionaries go to pagan areas, people there do not need any teaching on the reality of demons. They are well acquainted with the existence of evil spirits. They recognize or perceive their presence through certain symptoms manifested by the victim. The most common of these are:

1. Physical difficulties. Luke 13:11 speaks of a spirit of infirmity. "*A woman was there who had been crippled by a spirit for eighteen years. She was bent over and could not straighten up at all.*"When a spirit of infirmity has been resident in a person for a period of time, physical damage is usually done to the body so that even when the spirit is cast out, the person will still appear to be crippled or whatever. Thus it is important to pray for healing as well as deliverance.

2. Ungodly beliefs. Any amount of involvement in any philosophy or practice that does not point to the one true God is an open door to demonic interference in a person's life and can be recognized by affiliation with cults, false religions, the occult and errors in theology.

3. Emotional and mental problems. When certain emotions such as hatred, bitterness, inferiority and the like begin to dominate a personality to such an extent that they become recognizable characteristics of the person, demonic involvement is legitimately suspect. People who mean to be organized but consistently spin their tires in the mire of procrastination should request prayer for deliverance, as should those who feel confused much of the time or those whose memory seems clouded by a thick grey fog.

4. Lack of control of the tongue. Few things are uglier than gossip emanating from the mouth of a Christian. Unfortunately, few things are more common. Satan loves to find an area of weakness and move his agents in. When one expects to hear gossip from someone, he should suspect demonic influence. If a person cannot be involved with others without finding something to criticize, or his words cannot be trusted because he has been discovered in lies so often, there should be no surprise in suspecting the presence of a spirit of gossip, a critical spirit, a lying spirit or whatever.

Isaiah 28:11 tells of the Lord speaking to His people through stammering lips. That is different than the stammer one often associates with a psychological problem but which is actually quite often a spiritual problem.

5. Compulsions. When doors have been opened for demonic entry and things like spirits of anxiety, fear or sexual impurity have taken up residence, they may be perceived through observation of compulsive behaviours such as addiction to alcohol, food, drugs or nicotine, or uncontrollable thoughts or behaviours in regard to sex, such as masturbation, perversions, adultery and incest, to name a few.

TOOLS OF THE TRADE

Going into battle can be a pretty scary thing. When the government sends our native sons overseas to battle, our boys go in with nothing but the best. They know that they carry finely tooled armaments. They know that when they load the ammunition into the barrel and pull the trigger there is going to be a big bang. Their combat gear reflects the latest technological advances in fibre development, design and protection. In some ways, earthly battle is more easily approached than spiritual warfare because the men and women who cross the seas can see exactly what they're dealing with in terms of attire, weapons and enemy. Every aspect of spiritual warfare, on the other hand, is taken by faith.

One of the most helpful elements in running toward the enemy is confidence - confidence that his shots cannot penetrate your armour and confidence that your shots will penetrate his. Thus two of the most important considerations are what to wear and what weapons to take.

1. What to wear: Ephesians 6:14-17 outlines the regulation attire for anyone doing spiritual battle:

> belt of truth buckled around the waist
> breastplate of righteousness in place
> feet fitted with the readiness that comes from the gospel of peace
> shield of faith to extinguish the flaming arrows
> helmet of salvation
> sword of the spirit (the Word of God)

For those who wonder why we're not given any armour for our backs, I guess it's because God expects us to be always moving forward. He will bring up the rear guard.

Some people tell cute little stories about how they get up every morning and put the armour on. Once we volunteer for active duty in the Lord's army, the armour of God should never be removed. Think about it. If the belt of truth comes off, what replaces it? - a lie? If righteousness comes off, what's left? - an unredeemed heart totally open to the wiles of Satan. Without the armour of God in place, where is the real Christianity?

2. The weapons of our warfare: 2 Cor. 10:4 says that, *"The weapons we fight with are not the weapons of the world. On the contrary, they have divine power to demolish strongholds"*. What are these weapons that will *"demolish arguments and every pretension that sets itself up against the knowledge of God"*? We touched on them in Chapter Three. They are:

> the Blood of Jesus (Rev. 12:10,11)
> the Name of Jesus (Acts 16:18, Mark 16:17)
> the Word of God (John 8:28,29)
> praise (Acts16:25,26)
> praying in tongues (Eph.6:18)
> fasting (Matt.17:21, Isaiah 58)

anointed music (IKings 3;15)
the gift of discerning of spirits (I Cor.12:10)
the word of our testimony (Rev.12:11)

WHAT TO EXPECT

Any soldier going into battle wonders what is ahead. What is the enemy going to do? How will the enemy react to his or her advances?

The same questions come to mind going into deliverance ministry. Are there going to be manifestations? What will I do if there are? Should I permit manifestations? Can I stop them? Will I be in danger? Am I going to look like a fool? Is someone going to get angry with me for standing up to demons?

Possibly. Don't worry. At times. Yes. No. Who cares and who cares.

The big problem with deliverance is the manifestations. When one is healed it is a beautiful time of sharing God's graciousness with deeply grateful, often very excited, people. Everyone loves to see a healing. On the other hand, anyone who tries to see what is going on during a deliverance is regarded as somewhat of a carnal weirdo. What normal person wants to see anyone vomit or watch someone undergoing twisted contortions of the body?

I have talked with people in the deliverance ministry who claim to allow no manifestations in their ministry. They say that when spirits are bound, there is no need for manifestations. In our experience, this position makes no sense.

When Jesus cast spirits out, Scripture records numerous instances of loud, messy releases. Mark 9:26 records, *"The spirit shrieked, convulsed him violently and came out. The boy looked so much like a corpse that many said, "He's dead". But Jesus took him by the hand and lifted him to his feet, and he stood up."*

Again in Mark 1:25,26 when the demonized man in the synagogue addressed Jesus, Jesus sternly commanded him to be quiet and commanded the spirit to come out of him. *"The evil spirit shook the man violently and came out of him with a shriek."*

Manifestations do not need to be either feared or shunned. They are simply very natural occurrences as people are set free.

A true deliverance should be a time of rejoicing in victory. We have seen people who have been witnesses to deliverance enter into salvation through seeing the reality of God's power over evil.

Although we should regard manifestations as natural and do not need to be disturbed by them, at the same time it is very important neither to encourage them nor to desire them. Satan deserves no stage. If it becomes apparent that things are happening for effect or attention, the spirits must be commanded to cease in the Name of Jesus. Only God must get any glory during deliverance.

Just as every salvation and every healing is unique, so is every deliverance. Some people are gloriously delivered without feeling or manifesting a thing. They simply believe that Jesus has delivered them in response to prayer and warfare and they go on to see lovely changes in their lives.

Some experience definite but mild signs that something has definitely happened. They may yawn, cough, burp, sigh, feel a release of tension or something similar.

Those who are released with very marked manifestations can experience some embarrassment or trauma at the time, but in retrospect they invariably view their experiences positively because they know without a shadow of a doubt that they have been set free. We have seen people pull back in times of extreme manifestations and refuse to continue the fight. However, very often we see that the higher the cost, the more wonderful the results. Those who are willing to see the discomfort through are never sorry.

Those in ministry who refuse to allow manifestations sometimes do people a very grave disservice. In their quest for respectability or sometimes in an honest desire to keep Satan from getting any attention, they force people to keep spirits stuffed inside. Usually people can control the spirits from manifesting in the initial stage of the deliverance, but when they do, they often actually prevent them from leaving and send them deeper into hiding.

For instance, it is not uncommon for a person to feel the pressure of the spirit coming up into the throat, seeking an exit through the mouth. If the person being delivered is praying out loud, saying the Name of Jesus or pleading the Blood of Jesus audibly, the spirit may retreat and hide deeper because it cannot face the Name of Jesus. Although I don't have a scriptural reference for this, I know that it is true, because I have had it happen. In such times, the person ministering deliverance needs to continue the warfare and instruct the counselee to pray silently.

Of course we have all seen the opposite extremes where, as soon as someone feels stirrings within, he or she begins to do all sorts of crazy things, thus playing right into Satan's hands and cooperating with the very things that need to be routed. Those situations need to be taken firmly in hand - but not squelched to the point where the person him/herself feels rejection. There simply needs to be a little bit of teaching on paying more attention to the leading of the Holy Spirit than the leading of the evil one. It is very important no matter what the circumstances of the deliverance that the person who is being delivered

needs to feel God's great love for him or her throughout the process.

WHO CAN DRIVE OUT DEMONS?

In any country the citizens are all subject to a particular
body of law which has been formulated by politicians
according to a particular philosophy. Law enforcers
are appointed to the work of making sure that the law
is upheld and courts are established to interpret the
laws and to bring justice to bear.

Each citizen has a particular function within the society, whether it be window-washer, doctor, hairdresser,
pastor, fireman, policeman or judge. Although each
person is equal in citizenship rights and privileges, not
all are given the job of enforcing the law. Policemen do
that.

There are times, however, when 'stuff happens', there
is nary a policeman to be found for miles and ordinary
citizens have to be prepared to become enforcers of
the law.

For instance, suppose Jack, Bill and Tom are fishing far
out in the wilderness. Jack catches a huge fish. Bill
wants the fish and so he hits Jack over the head with
an oar and kills him. Tom knows the law well enough
to know that murder is against the law. He also knows
that according to the law, he has the power and the
responsibility to make a citizen's arrest of Bill. Although he is a mechanic by trade, he tells Bill that he
is under arrest and takes him back to civilization where
he hands him over to the judge for justice to be done.
I realize that this is a 'fishy' story, but it serves to
illustrate the point that although not all Christians are
called into the deliverance ministry, we all have the
same power and authority to carry out the work of the
Kingdom of God and we need to be ready to go into
action if a situation presents itself. It also serves to

169

underline the responsibility that each of us has to know what God's Word says and how to apply it.

When trained, appointed law enforcers are available, it only makes sense that a citizen would request that a professional look after a situation. Otherwise, he might find himself quickly over his depth. In the same way, when a situation requiring deliverance arises, if an experienced spiritual warrior is available, people of other callings should defer to the experienced one in terms of leadership but remain as prayer support.

In the event that a citizen is personally harassed or effected by a lawbreaker, he needs to know that he has the right to protection by the law and he needs to know where to go for help. It is one thing to protect and recover one's own property from thieves, but it is another thing entirely to join the army of the country and set out to liberate all who are held captive by the enemy. While there are similarities in the basic principle, the strategies are entirely different. In the same way, standing against Satan in one's own life is good preparation for ministering deliverance to others but there are differences to consider.

Anyone who confronts Satan and takes authority over him on behalf of another person, needs to be prepared for the fact that there is more to deliverance than just casting a demon out. The person may need prayer for healing of the damage inflicted upon the body or the emotions by the spirit. Discernment and sensitivity to the leading of the Lord is very important.

Another consideration for anyone considering whether or not to involve him or herself in deliverance is the cost involved. So many people know that they need to be set free and yet cannot find anyone who will pray in faith and cast demons out with authority. When someone's name begins to surface as a reputable and effective administrator of deliverance, people come from far and wide for help. Demonized people need a lot of attention. We are basically on call twenty-four hours a day. Reputable surgeons would never operate and then throw a person to the wind to fend for him or herself. Neither do we.

Usually the person who is delivered has a change in personality traits and may find the adjustment to new emotions free from impediments somewhat strange. He or she may become hesitant and call for advice. Until a person becomes strong in knowing how to fend off attacks of Satan, he or she may need a great deal of support. A clear mind feels good, but it can take some adjustment.

The time and energy commitment is great, not only in ministry, but also in personal prayer, Scripture reading and Christian fellowship in order to stay strong. Of course the cost involved in being faced with accusations of all kinds is another serious consideration, because Satan will try to discredit anyone who dares invade his territory.

Mark 16:17, *"And these signs will accompany those who believe: in My Name they will drive out demons"*, is a pretty clear profile on who can drive out demons. Simply - believers.

Thus every believer can administer deliverance and has the right to practice it. However, not everyone is called to the deliverance ministry. I believe that unless it is an emergency, those who do not have that specific ministry should stay out of the way, pray and support those who have been called to the front lines, encourage burdened souls to seek deliverance and direct them to an effective ministry.

HOW TO GO FORTH INTO BATTLE

For some reason, formulas don't seem to work too well in the Kingdom of God. Just when one thinks he has God figured out, something happens to remind him of the boundlessness of God's creativity and His absolutely individual approach to each precious life. Telling someone what words to say or formulating a template prayer is for the most part meaningless. It's not about saying the right things. It's about having the right 'heart condition'. If a person's heart is right before God and if God sends him or her to do a job, then He will equip that person with the right words for the occasion.

The main things to remember are to:
1. stand firm on the Word of God,
2. make sure your armour is intact,
3. ask God to cover you with the Blood of Jesus for protection,
4. depend on Jesus to do the work and remember that He is the Deliverer.

The best anyone can do in teaching another how to administer deliverance is to point people to the examples in Scripture and share what seems to be most effective from personal experience.

There are times when, in a prayer line or wherever, we simply command a spirit to "come out in the Name of Jesus" and release happens immediately. There are times when we never see that person again but often hear through contact with the person or a friend that God did a great work.

Other times, as we have already mentioned, if someone comes to one of our meetings and it becomes obvious that serious deliverance is needed, rather than attempting any quick fix, we bind the strong man (Satan) from further interference in the person's life until the spirits are cast out and make an appointment to meet privately with the person and a prayer team.

Binding and Loosing: In Matt. 12:29, when Jesus was teaching His disciples about deliverance, He asked, *"How can anyone enter a strong man's house and carry off his possessions unless he first ties up the strong man? Then he can rob his house."* In Matt. 16:19, He said, *"I will give you the keys of the Kingdom of Heaven: whatever you bind on earth will be bound in Heaven, and whatever you loose on earth will be loosed in Heaven."*

If you retain only one thing from this book, retain this: In the original Greek, this verse is written with different tenses than interpreted in our English translations. It is written thusly: *"I will give thee the keys of the Kingdom of the Heavens and whatever thou bindest on the earth shall be **having been bound in the heavens** and whatever thou loosest on the earth shall be **having been loosed in the heavens."***

Here God is not saying that He will simply endorse our actions. Our actions, guided by the Holy Spirit, will be in accordance with the Heavenly Pattern! The work has already been accomplished.

When we bind the strong man in a person's life, we simply appropriate for that person what has already been provided for him or her in Heaven. When we pray, we simply turn the key in the lock that opens the door to God's blessings and provision for us. We are key turners! Praise God!!!

The whole thing about deliverance is that it is God's work and He has already accomplished it! We simply need to reach out and receive. As readers, I hope that you can get as excited about this as I am writing it!

We fight from the position of victory! When we fight to get the victory, we've lost it from the beginning. When we feel that we need great power to overcome Satan, it's often just that Satan is trying to lift himself up in our minds. He has been defeated.

In practical terms, when we bind the evil one and loose God's child, it is a declaration that we make to Satan and the wording is not according to any formula, but according to the words that the Holy Spirit gives to us at the time. Sometimes we repeat the binding several times and sometimes we make only one declaration. Our declaration might go something like this:

In the Name of Jesus we bind all of the works of darkness in the life of_____ . We tie you so tightly that you can no longer move in this life. We render you powerless through the Blood of Jesus. We remind you that you have been defeated through the death and resurrection of Jesus Christ. You are bound until such time as you are completely cast out of this life. We command you to release this child of God now in the Name of Jesus.

When we meet privately - Because Jesus tells us in Matthew 18:19 that, *"If two of you on Earth agree about anything you ask for, it will be done for you by My Father in Heaven. For where two or three come together in My Name, there am I with them"*, we like to meet people with a prayer team of two or three people who we know believe God and can be trusted in absolute confidentiality.

Before the person is scheduled to arrive, we spend time in prayer asking the Lord to cleanse us personally. We ask Him to forgive us for our own sins, to give us discernment, to direct the meeting and to cover us with the Blood of Jesus, thus protecting us from the evil one and any spirits which may want to do us harm. Again we bind any spirits which may be associated with the person so that they cannot interfere with the deliverance. For instance, there have been times when a person with an appointment begins to feel very ill or gets a terrible headache and calls to cancel the meeting.

When a person arrives, we encourage him or her to be comfortable and we pray a brief initial prayer asking the Lord to be with us.

As we relax and get to know each other a bit, we simply chat, encouraging the person to share areas of his or her life which may have been entry points for a troublesome spirit. For some this may be a long, drawn out process while others are able to briefly pinpoint areas of concern. Whatever the scenario, it is extremely important to be focused, compassionate, interested listeners during this time of sharing.

Before going into prayer, we talk to the person a bit about deliverance and what he may expect. We tell him that if he hears us speaking forcefully or whatever, we're not angry with him, we are simply dealing with things in the spirit realm. We reassure him that there is no need to be embarrassed about anything that might happen, because we know that any strange manifestations have nothing to do with him, but are simply the spirits which may fight to stay. We suggest that if he feels anything happening to him at any stage that he lets us know so that we can better deal with it.

In spite of the fact that the person may claim to be a Christian, when we sense from the Holy Spirit that it is time to move on from the sharing into prayer, we lead the person in a prayer of recommitment of his life to Jesus Christ, acknowledging Him as the Supreme Being and thanking God for sending His Son and His precious Holy Spirit. We then lead him to renounce all evil and everything in which he has been involved that is not of God. We lead him to ask God to forgive him of his sins and then thank Him for His forgiveness. Following that, we have him take authority over everything he is aware of that is not of God and rebuke things that he recognizes as being wrongfully present. For instance, suppose that we were working with a girl named Jane. She might have come because she couldn't control her eating and despite trying every diet counselling scheme in the book, she was driven to eat.

Jane recognizes the fruit of the problem - the overeating, but she knows that there must be a root that is producing this problem in her life.

We would lead Jane in a declaration of her authority over every spirit causing her to overeat and instruct her to rebuke those spirits. Following her declaration of her will to be free from those spirits, we would further declare to Satan that, "Jane has renounced her gluttony and we take authority in the Name of Jesus over every spirit associated with that practice".

Because we have often found rejection, self-pity, resentment, frustration, anxiety and various kinds of fears to be associated with gluttony, we would name some of those and call them out. If a particular one elicited some form of reaction, such as shaking, fluttering of the eyes, twitching or something unusual, we would probably ask Jane what was happening inside. She might claim to feel as though she was being choked or experiencing something unusual.

With that, we would go after the thing that was named, perhaps the spirit of rejection. We would command it out in the Name of Jesus. As we audibly rebuked the various spirits, we would encourage Jane to agree with us silently in prayer. We would continue to pressure that spirit to come out until it did.

One by one, as the Holy Spirit led us to focus on a particular spirit, we would cast them out.

As we rebuke the spirits, we usually speak in a normal tone of voice. There is no need to yell at demons unless the Holy Spirit for some reason impresses one to do so. It is important to remain calm and so we would continue to reassure Jane that everything was going to be all right. We never curse or ridicule demons. 2 Peter 2:10,11 warns, *"Bold and arrogant, these men are not afraid to slander celestial beings, yet even angels, although they are stronger and more powerful, do not bring slanderous accusations against such beings in the presence of the Lord"*.

Demons usually leave through the mouth through yawning, burping, coughing screaming or whatever, although that is not always true. They seem to be able to exit through any part of the body including the skin. If we worked with Jane for a couple of hours and it became apparent that there was a lot more work to be done but that she herself was tiring, we might suggest that we break for a few days and make another appointment. It is difficult for people to join into aggressive warfare when they are tired.

Before she left, however, we would ask if she was feeling any sort of pressure anywhere and rebuke the source of that pressure so that she would leave with a feeling of encouragement rather than heaviness.

On the other hand, if Jane felt that the work was complete and that she was entirely free, we would encourage her to call if she had any questions and instruct her on how to stay free. We would also brief her on the principles of self-deliverance so that she would not have to depend on us if she were to run into further trouble.

SELF DELIVERANCE

It is not necessary to run to someone else for prayer every time one discovers an intrusion of the enemy. The principles for self-deliverance basically follow the same pattern as the principles for praying for someone else to be set free.

1. Go to Jesus who is the deliverer.
2. Confess any area of transgression. and request forgiveness.
3. Submit yourself entirely to His will.
4. Know that you are in a position of victory over the enemy and that your responsibility is simply to appropriate Christ's victory rather than "win the battle".
5. Take authority in the Name of Jesus and rebuke anything that is not of God.
6. Know that the enemy has to leave.
7. Claim back the ground stolen by Satan. Be aggressive.
8. Be sensitive to the leading of the Holy Spirit in leading you to clean up other areas.
9. Don't give up. Be persistent in breaking bondages.
10. Thank God for what He has done in your life.
11. Be diligent in maintaining your freedom and keeping the doors or entry points closed.

PRACTICAL SUGGESTIONS

I always think that it's interesting to watch boxers as they first enter a ring. Like elastic bands stretched to the max they vibrate in their respective corners, shouts of advice hammering into their ears as they wait for the bell. Sizing up their opponents with lowered heads and slitted eyes they do the intimidation thing to the best of their ability. As the bell sounds, out they come, chins down, lefts up, dancing that fancy little boxer's two step, trying a jab here, a little jab there, looking for the big opening.

As people who find themselves called upon to administer deliverance, I think that we sometimes do too much dancing around, trying to get a handle on our opponent, taking little jabs here and little jabs there, instead of getting into the ring like the champions we are and packing that knock out punch.

I believe that much of the problem stems from lack of experience and the uncertainty that comes with insufficient example. So few people administer deliverance that there are very few people from whom to learn. The following are a few practical suggestions from our years of experience in seeing people set free.

1. **Be flexible**. Although we like to meet with people privately when we know that there is a need for deliverance, there are times when we have to deal with situations in public meetings. Jesus certainly did not require people who needed immediate deliverance to set up an appointment with His secretary. Many pastors are afraid of disturbance in their services, but if the Holy Spirit is leading, I would much rather have a display of His power to deliver than to know that I've quenched the Spirit in my requirement for "respectability".

2. **Get rid of the notion that deliverance should be a dark little secret**. In times of prayer at an altar, if the Lord gives you discernment, don't be afraid to pray as you are led. Otherwise, you are shortchanging people who come desiring freedom from their burdens. Be as ready to pray for deliverance as you are for healing. Remember Psalm 103:2. *"Bless the Lord, Oh my soul, and forget not all His benefits"*. Deliverance is a benefit offered freely by God.

Pastors of medium to large congregations cannot possibly look after every individual need in a congregation, but Jesus can if given the opportunity. Group prayer for release of individual burdens should be a regular part of every meeting.

179

3. **Don't force yourself on people who are unwilling to seek deliverance, but do force the Name of Jesus on spirits who are unwilling to leave**. Before people can receive deliverance, they must request it of their own free will. No matter how concerned one person may be for another, any pushing will simply be counterproductive.

If, however, someone has requested prayer and the spirits within him or her speaks out saying something like, "I don't want to do this anymore", or "I want you to stop this", recognize the source of the resistance, bind the spirit from hindering deliverance and command it to leave in the Name of Jesus.

4. **Try not to pray for people of the opposite sex unless you have a member of the opposite sex on your prayer team**. We find that working together as a married couple is the optimum situation. We balance each other. As we drive and do the incidental things of life together, we have an opportunity to discuss people's needs without breaking any confidences, thereby gaining a wider perspective on individual cases.

No one these days should have to be reminded of the dangers of going solo in counselling a member of the opposite sex.

5. **Avoid getting into any discussion with a demon**. We occasionally ask a spirit to name itself. However, the only recorded instance where this was done in Scripture was Mark 5:9 where Jesus spoke to the man in the region of the Gerasenes and asked the evil spirit to name itself. The response was, *"My name is Legion"*, which would seem to signify a large grouping rather than any particular spirit. The very idea of conversing with a demon is like blowing into

180

the wind. If Satan is the father of lies, why on earth would we think that anything a demon might have to say should be trusted?

Is it not much better to ask the Holy Spirit who promises to lead us into all truth to reveal the nature of the spirit to us and then call that nature out? We often find that by asking the person what they are hearing inside we can discover what lurks there and call it out.

6. Remember that warfare is different from prayer. Prayer is communication with our Heavenly Father. Warfare involves declarations made in the Name of Jesus to Satan according to the provisions of the cross.

CHAPTER ELEVEN

SUFFER THE LITTLE CHILDREN

"Pastor Del Zotto?" The female voice on the other end of the line sounded very tense and shaky.

"Yes", I responded.

"This is Lilly _____ and I've heard about you praying for people to get rid of evil spirits. Do you ever pray for children?", she quavered. When I told her that we have prayed for many little ones, I could hear an audible sigh of relief.

She proceeded to tell me that she was at the end of her rope with her three year old son. She said that he was extremely hyperactive and difficult to handle. She told me about taking him to doctor after doctor and finding nothing but intensified anxiety. As we spoke, the hope of help arose in her heart and she began to weep as months of frustration broke within her. She made an appointment to bring Cody, her child, to see us.

Before they arrived, we prayed that God would give us discernment and direction.

With his curly mop of golden brown curls, Cody had an adorable appearance, but that was the only adorable part of him! From the moment he set foot in my office, there was trouble. That child was into everything. However, we made a fuss over the little fellow and attempted to get to know him a bit.

He wasn't interested. He had to check out everything that could be seen and had no shyness about hunting for things that couldn't be seen. He chattered to himself the whole time, occasionally declaring, "I'm a little devil, I'm a little devil!" For the first ten minutes or so, Lilly chased him and apologized for his behaviour.

Finally, when we'd gotten the picture, I suggested to Lilly that she bring Cody over to me. When I attempted to take him on my knee, He began to kick and squirm and fuss like a hellion. I had quite a time trying to keep him on my knee, but felt that it was important to hold him so that we could pray over him.

Without frightening the little boy, we bound the spirits and commanded them to stop harassing the child immediately.

Cody quieted down right away and sat happily on my lap. I asked him why he was running around saying that he was a little devil.

"My Mommy calls me that. She says I'm a little devil", he replied with a cocky little smile.

Lilly admitted with some embarrassment that she did have a bad habit of calling Cody a little devil. She went on to say that, in their culture, it was normal to take a hyperactive child like Cody to one of the religious men of the family for special rituals and that she had done that. As I questioned her about the rituals and she elaborated on the practices, it became apparent that witchcraft was involved. Of course Lilly had had no idea that these traditions which had been practised in her culture for many, many generations had anything to do with witchcraft. She was shocked that I should suggest such a thing.

When people are desperate, it's not unusual for them to grasp at anything that promises relief. Satan counts on desperation for a lot of his business. He has no qualms whatsoever about taking advantage of frightened people in all manner of pain. Taking advantage of ignorance is like taking candy from a baby for him.

 After instructing Lilly to never call Cody a little devil again and pointing her to Proverbs 11:9, 12:18, 15:4 and 18:21 where the power of the tongue is shown to curse or bless our children, we encouraged her to call on God who is full of mercy and love rather than relying on rituals in times of distress. Then we prepared to pray.

By this time, Cody was getting pretty restless. We quietly but firmly commanded the demons to leave in the Name of Jesus and to the amazement of everyone, that beautiful little boy stopped his fussing immediately, relaxed, curled up in my lap, snuggled into my arm, closed his little eyes and fell into a peaceful sleep. We all smiled at one another and gave great thanks to God for His blessing.

PARENTAL RESPONSIBILITY

When a child is born into a family, that child is entrusted by God to the parents for its raising. To many parents, clean clothing, adequate food, regular Sunday School, a bike at Christmas and the odd trip to Disneyland signifies a good job, well done.

There's more.

It is during the formative years when children are vulnerable that many of the struggles that can dog them for life begin. Parents need to make themselves very aware of possible entry points for demonic interference and study the Scriptures so that they know what the promises of God really are.

The vast majority of parents with whiny, obnoxious children simply struggle through the days, trying to make it until bedtime without losing control of themselves, having no idea of the struggles within those dear little children which can often be prayed away.

Because God has entrusted the children to their parents and has given them His Word as a textbook for their care, it is the responsibility of the parents to shield their little ones from the attacks of the evil one, keeping them covered in prayer. By submitting the family to the Lordship of Jesus Christ and making every effort to follow Him, the entire family can rest under the umbrella of God's protection. When the parents allow quarrelling, strife and mean spirits to enter their relationship, it removes their protective covering and leaves their children open to demonic attack by spirits of fear, insecurity, resentment, rebellion, hatred and the like. If not routed, these things can impose misery on the children and all of their future relationships and on down through succeeding generations.

Thanks be to God that provision has been made for restoration.

Once the parents realize what they have done by allowing the removal of the umbrella, they can go to God, asking forgiveness of their selfish, ungodly behaviour, ask Him to make them sensitive to how to pray for their children, take authority over the areas He illumines, take back the ground stolen by Satan and determine to shield their children from further intrusion of the evil one.

"BUT I DEDICATED MY CHILD TO GOD!"

I have heard parents scoff at the very idea of any spiritual problems with their children on the basis of having Dedicated their children to God.

There has been a lot of misunderstanding about Dedication. A Dedication service is more a service of commitment of the parents to raising the children in the nurture and admonition of the Lord than it is an insurance policy on protection for the child.

If it weren't so pathetic it would be laughable to see some of these great looking parents who bring their well scrubbed, designer clad children for Dedication, smile and receive all of the congratulations from the

186

congregation and then put the dear little baby in the car seat for the ride home and "get real". The smiles come off. Some little annoyance may be verbally thrust into the air and caught by the mate. Then it starts. Cutting little comments escalate to loud, verbal bricks thrown to inflict as much emotional pain as possible. In total frustration, Mommy punches the side of Daddy's head as he drives. In pain and blinding anger, he lashes back.

Meanwhile, the little one in the back, gazing out the car window watching all of the trees and houses go by, is strangling in a black cloud of insecurity, meanness, self-centredness, rejection, resentment and misery, to name a few of the feelings that can be entry points for spirits of the same nature. If he or she dares to whimper, whine or cry, the response is often impatience or angry frustration. The little one soon learns that it's better to be quiet, endure and just stuff the pain way down inside.

As Susie gets a little older, Mommy and Daddy wonder why on earth she keeps throwing temper tantrums. At least they know it's nothing spiritual because Susie was Dedicated to God.

As the pretty baby grows into a pretty teenager, the things she stuffed way down inside as a baby begin to surface - rejection, fear, hatred, loneliness, resentment. Because she's growing up and feeling a bit more powerful than she did as a child, she tests the possibilities of releasing and expressing the pressures of the grunge inside. Of course the results aren't good. Who's going to react positively to a teenager who rejects authority, hates her parents, resents offerings of advice and thinks of no one but herself? And so, because her relationships are much too painful to handle, she tries to stuff everything down inside again. This time they won't stay hidden quite so well and so she tries some stuffing tools - food, alcohol, drugs, sex - whatever works and seems to suit her lifestyle.

The frantic parents, white knuckled from wringing their hands, run into the Pastor's office. "Why is Susie rebelling like this? What is wrong with her? She's hooking and stealing to get money for her drugs. We Dedicated her to God!"

Poor children. Poor parents. Poor fools.

A child who is raised in an atmosphere of negative tensions will invariably be left open to demonic harassment.

PREVENTATIVE MEDICINE

Happy the child whose parents have the wisdom and selflessness to settle their differences with prayer, set and consistently maintain firm boundaries, deal with any negative emotions before they become spiritual problems and go to the Lord for restoration of the umbrella when they've fallen flat on their faces.

FATHER-GOD, FATHER-DADDY

Why not just eliminate the problem of spousal tensions from the child rearing arena and opt for divorce, separating the father, the mother and the children?

That's like suggesting a separation of the Trinity - the Father, the Holy Spirit and the Son.

We are made in the image of God, not only in our individual beings, but in that most foundational unit of society - the family. Each has its function in individuality and yet are one.

It's true that husbands and wives often seem to be a lot more aggravation and trouble than they're worth. I've heard it said that marriage is the cruelest thing that God ever did to mankind. I imagine that if a magnificent wooden carving could talk about the carpenter who fashioned it, it would say the same thing about sandpaper, and yet without the sandpaper, the carving could never have been a magnificent thing.

Marriage can be grossly painful when lived in an environment of self-centredness. God-centred marriage, on the other hand, is one of the most precious experiences imaginable. The need for sanding comes in where God-centredness is forgotten in favour of self-centredness.

Rightly viewed, marriage is a process of replacing self-centredness with other-centredness and God-centredness. After submitting to the pain of sanding, the whole family will reap rich rewards.

Proverbs 14:1 says, *"The wise woman builds her house, but with her own hands the foolish one tears hers down"*. While a man scripturally has the responsibility of guarding his home, providing for his family and taking the spiritual leadership as priest, a woman seems to be more responsible for building the structures within it. If she tears at the relationships, emotionally or physically dividing her children from their father, the father from the children, the children from each other or separating herself from any of them, the Bible calls her a fool. Her end will be a pathetic, lonely sea of bitterness.

The only commandment with a promise is the one about honouring parents: *"Honour your father and your mother, so that you may live long in the land"*. Both fathers and mothers need to realize that children's understanding of God as Father is built on the image they see of the father in their home. Thus it is of the utmost importance to the healthy growth of a child that the father conduct himself with wisdom, love, justice and mercy and that the mother do everything she can to foster this image of the father in the eyes of the children. If she does not show respect for the child's father, why would the child? If the child grows to disrespect the father, he or she will be robbed of the blessing of God. Any perverse motivation the mother may have in leading a child to disrespect the father will backfire on her as the child grows to disrespect her as well.

Of course no one is perfect. No father is going to perfectly model God for any child. However, it is his responsibility to try his best and to ask forgiveness of his family when he fails. A wise mother will shield the children as much as possible from the faults of the father and build their image of him on his positive points.

If the wife, in spite of the husband's shortcomings, nurtures her children to respect their father according to the commandments, the whole family will be blessed and the father will gradually grow into the place of being worthy of respect. Meanwhile, along the way, the children will have received a minimum of damage.

What does all of this have to do with deliverance?

If a child grows with an unhealthy view of the father, it is much more difficult for him or her to respond to God the Father in later years. If a father has been preoccupied, judgmental, critical and aloof, his children will find it hard to approach God. Deep in their hearts they will feel too discouraged to sincerely consider the possibility that God would value them enough to listen let alone free them from the pain of their lives.

"An ounce of prevention is worth a pound of cure" - or so the saying goes. If a child has been raised to love and respect the earthly father and has been trained in the ways of the Lord, obedience to His Word will come naturally, thus saving him or her from many of the pitfalls of disobedience which Satan loves to use as entry points.

WORDS OF DEATH - WORDS OF LIFE

"Come on, Greg. It's eleven o'clock and I've already called you four times. You're as lazy as a pet coon." Mom huffs and slams Greg's door in exasperation. Greg turns over, thinks about a fat, furry animal curled up asleep in the trunk of a tree somewhere and associates himself with it. If Mom says he's lazy, then he must be.

A couple of days later, Dad asks him to help with the garage clean-up. Into Greg's sub-conscious pops the image of the lazy old coon curled up in the tree trunk. "Yea, Dad. I'll be there." On the way to the garage, he passes the T.V. which just happens to be on. He gets a bit involved and before long is totally immersed in the program, sub-consciously feeling legitimate in his behaviour. After all, He's supposed to be lazy. He knows that the only consequence will be irritated parents. So what?

Eventually, after inviting the label of laziness a number of times, as Greg goes deeper into agreement with the concept of his laziness, a spirit of fatigue shows up with a few associates like tiredness, procrastination, passivity, weariness and slothfulness and they attach themselves to Greg. From the point of allowing a transgression of the flesh, Greg has progressed to the point where he is no longer able to control his laziness. His problem is now a spiritual problem rather than an easily rectified, natural problem of the flesh.

How could this have been avoided?

Greg should have known the night before what time he was expected to be up in the morning. He should have had an alarm clock and been responsible for fulfilling his parents' expectations. He should have known the night before what the consequences of sleeping late would be and known beyond a shadow of a doubt that those consequences would be carried out.

However, since that was obviously not the case, Greg's Mom should have made sure somehow, even if it meant throwing cold water on him, that Greg got up the first time she called. It was her sloppy parenting that started the problem.

What needs to happen now?

Greg's Mom needs to speak words of life into her son's spirit by asking him to forgive her for speaking negative attributes into his life. He needs to confess his lack of response to her as sin, ask God to forgive him, renounce laziness and all other associated spirits and then make sure that whenever he's tempted to be lazy he forces himself to do what needs to be done.

Will this happen?

Not likely. That's why it is so important for parents to be very careful about each word they speak to their children. Are they speaking words of life - or are they speaking words of death? Children need to be guided into responsible adulthood through loving, consistent setting and maintaining of boundaries and expectations. It's not fair for children to be made vulnerable to Satan's ploys through sloppy parenting.

Over and over again we pray for people who have been bound by spirits of rejection, failure and the like because of parents who have told them over and over again that they are never going to amount to anything.

PUTTING AWAY CHILDISH THINGS

When Johnny comes home from school complaining about Mark and Danny calling him a jerk, Mom and Dad could be tempted to sluff the complaint off, thinking that it's just one of those childish things.

However, if Johnny has remembered it and has verbalized the humiliation to his parents, chances are he's asking for some help, some release from his confusion and pain.

It's very important for parents to be sensitive to needs that their children bring to their attention, no matter how trivial they may seem at the time. The children need to know that their concerns matter to the parents. They need to be taught through example to have healthy responses to those around them. When it seems that there could be an entry point of any kind, parents need to pray with their children, claiming freedom from any bondage Satan may be trying to impose.

ANGELS, WITCHES AND GOBLINS

Spiritual realities are no secret to children. They are very sensitive to moods, atmospheres and attitudes. These days, with occult cartoons, games, clothing and music assaulting their spirits, they need protection more than ever before.

Because they're so sensitive, they can easily be filled with fear about things they don't understand. It's a great comfort to them if they are gently taught that they have control over some of their scary thoughts. There's no need to get into heavy teaching about rebuking and binding and casting out demons with little ones. On the other hand, not teaching them that Satan exists does them a disservice. They need to know the source of bad things and that they don't need to worry about them as long as they stay close to Jesus. It is extremely important that Satan not be given any ground in their lives through unnecessary fears.

It's a beautiful thing when a child can grow in the security of knowing that he or she is able to tap into the love and power and promises of the Lord Jesus Christ at any moment, anywhere, in any circumstances.

WHEN AND HOW TO PRAY DELIVERANCE OVER CHILDREN

The question with children is whether to pray for them when they're awake or asleep.

If they're particularly restless or rebellious, it may be better to wait until they're sleeping. However, no matter when one prays, it's vital to remember that everything said over a child will go into his or her mind. Therefore, if more than one person is praying, it's important not to have any discussions about the child in his or her presence, because those conclusions and questions will enter the sub-conscious and possibly cause difficulties later.

If the child is sleeping, laying hands on the forehead as one speaks quietly against the enemy is sufficient to loose Satan's hold. One could pray thusly: "I command all spirits of rejection, rebellion, failure (or whatever the Lord indicates) to leave this child in the Name of Jesus. I loose him into obedience to Jesus. I set him totally free by the Blood of Jesus from the spirits that have been harassing him.

Praying Scripture back to God in a loving environment is a deeply healing thing to do over a child. Even though he or she may not be awake, those words going deep into his or her spirit will bring strength and new life.

CHAPTER TWELVE

LIVING IN THE LIGHT

"When an evil spirit comes out of a man, it goes through arid places seeking rest and does not find it. Then it says, 'I will return to the house I left'. When it arrives, it finds the house swept clean and put in order. Then it goes and takes seven other spirits more wicked than itself, and they go in and live there. And the final condition of the man is worse than the first." (Luke 11:26)

Let's just think about this for a moment.

Sandra is depressed. Very depressed. She wakes up each morning and tears begin to trickle onto the pillow as she thinks about having to begin another day. At the dinner table, her husband asks, "Would you please pass the salt?". Sandra begins to weep. Having no idea what to do with his wife, he asks, "What's wrong?" She sadly shakes her head and excuses herself. She has way of communicating the depth of sadness inside.

Sandra knows that she has to get a grip. She begins to walk each day. Exercise is supposed to be a great energy booster - but it's just another chore.

She goes to the local Naturopath with hope of finding an herbal remedy. Hundreds of dollars later, she is still weeping.

No problem. Sandra has a very good friend always available to comfort her - food. As soon as she is alone in the house, she walks to the frig, finds anything edible, sits at table in front of the T.V. and stuffs her pain with "Oprah" for company - day after agonizing day.

At two hundred and ten pounds, Sandra knows that

she has to find her way out of the black tunnel. She gets her family doctor to refer her to a psychiatrist who says he can't begin to help her until she goes on Prozac. Afraid of the side effects, she walks out of the clinic a hopeless blob of humanity not caring about the people who stare at her tears as she walks by.

Finally Sandra, a Christian for fifteen years, decides that as a last resort she will ask her pastor to pray deliverance over her. She holds nothing back as she pours her heart out to him. Almost weeping himself at the painful disclosures of her heart, he takes her hand and presents her needs before the Lord. Then, in the presence of the Holy Spirit and Sandra, he takes authority over the spirit of depression and commands it to leave in the Name of Jesus.

The demon inside cowers. It cannot stand that Name! It hides in a desperate hope that the young pastor is just repeating some words without any belief attached to them. But no! He's saying that Name again and he knows the Christ. In desperation to escape from the power in the Name of Jesus, the black spirit flees through Sandra's breath.

Sandra begins to cough and suddenly feels an over-whelming sense of peace. The heavy burden on her shoulders has lifted.

Her 'house' has been swept clean. The demon of depression has taken flight into dry places. Sandra's black tunnel has given way to light.

The demon suddenly finds itself a vagabond spirit, with no body through which to express its nature, cast into dry places. Oh, the agony of having no soul within which to dwell. Oh, the agony of separation. Oh, the agony, the agony. It searches and searches for another entry point through which to find rest, but can find nothing.

Along the way, it commiserates with other vagabond

spirits seeking rest. They drift together, first one joining Depression, then another, each one worse than the first.

Meanwhile, Sandra feels wonderful! She is so happy to be free of the heaviness. She has no more tears in the morning. Now she gets up early, watches "Sally Jessy Raphael", "Montel Williams", "Jerry Springer" and then "Jenny Jones". Lunch is great. She has leftover pizza from the night before in preparation for her afternoon with the soaps. Following an evening at the movies, she feels a twinge of guilt about not reading the Bible all day but - oh well - maybe tomorrow.

Sandra's house is swept clean, but it's empty. She doesn't even try to change her old destructive habits. The doors are wide open, awaiting whatever the wind may blow through.

Depression drifts by with the spirits of Suicide, Hopelessness, Insomnia, Morbidity, Despair, Gluttony, and Death. In unspeakable relief at finding the doors wide open and the Holy Spirit locked in a room in the centre of the house, they enter with glee.

In the middle of a soap opera ('Luke' just having deserted 'Laura' because he's passionately in love with 'Monica') Sandra begins to feel very sad. She thinks of how dull her life is in comparison with the soaps.

Quickly she begins a descent into despair. Hopelessness overwhelms her. She can't sleep at night and she eats all day. Soon her thoughts are consumed by thoughts of death and she imagines what she would look like in a casket. She begins to focus on thoughts of suicide and finally one day _____.

ALLOW THE HOLY SPIRIT TO FILL YOUR HOUSE

The only way that spirits can return is through human

failure to allow the Holy Spirit to fill the 'house'.

God's greatest desire is to be in such close relationship with us that His Holy Spirit fills not only our spirits (remember those three concentric circles?) but overflows throughout our souls and bodies, leaving no place for Satan.

At Salvation, Jesus comes into our hearts and fills our spirit with His Holy Spirit. He seals that spirit part of us. Ephesians 1:13,14 says, *"You also were included in Christ when you heard the Word of truth, the gospel of your Salvation. Having believed, you were marked in Him with a seal, the promised Holy Spirit, who is a deposit guaranteeing our inheritance until the redemption of those who are God's possession"*. It's like a glass being filled to the 'Spirit level'.

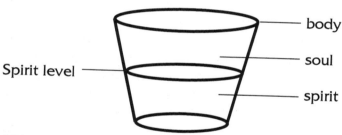

Although no demon can touch the spirit of a Christian, our souls and bodies remain unredeemed. As we grow in relationship with God and turn our minds, emotions, etc. more and more over to Him, the 'Spirit level' in the glass rises and we become more and more Spirit filled.

 As we are set free, we need to consciously yield the areas that have been freed to the Holy Spirit. Whatever areas are given to Him are impenetrable to Satan.

The illustration of the full glass of water totally immersed in a pail of water works well to communicate the ideal state of the Christian in relation to the indwelling, overflowing immersion of the Holy Spirit.

BE CHRIST-CONFIDENT, NOT SATAN-SHAKY

The illustration of Sandra's deliverance and subsequent worse state is not given for the purpose of inciting fear of Satan's return after a deliverence. It is simply an portrayal of what can happen if one does not hold fast to Christ after being set free.

One might say it is simply an example of Christian stupidity.

It's extremely important to remember that we are on the winning side.

Philippians 1:6 reassures us to be confident of this; *"that He who began a good work in you will carry it on to completion until the Day of Christ Jesus"*.

When there has been believing prayer (not simply words spoken in unbelief) and declaration of deliverance, one can hold fast to the fact that release really has happened.

What sometimes happens to cause doubt is that a person may be delivered from a spirit, perhaps a spirit of fear, but following a brief experience of freedom from fear, becomes bothered once again by anxieties etc. What has probably happened is that the person was in fact delivered of a spirit of fear, but other spirits of the same nature went into hiding and were not cast out at that time. The breaking of bondages is usually a progressive thing.

Thus, even though there has been a major deliverance, it is quite probable that there is still more freedom to be won.

BE COMMITTED

Upon the first opening of the eyelids in the morning, it is a lovely thing to stretch and say, "Good morning, Lord", in confident recognition of His presence.

A conscious daily commitment to choose His will over all temptations does not have to be made in an

199

attitude of sacrificial will power, but of wholehearted love and desire to be pleasing to Christ.

When the attitude of the heart is 'not my will but Thy will'; when the self seems unimportant beside the beauty of Christ, the dark spirits know that there's no point even looking for entry points.

SEEK GODLY COUNSEL

After one has been released from serious demonization, even though the mind is clear in the sense of lacking obstruction, it can be very confused as a result of prolonged dysfunctional responses.

If one has lived in hatred, fear and rejection for many years, knowing how to function normally may take a bit of wise counsel.

NEW HABITS - NEW FRIENDS

When people are delivered from smoking, they suddenly have nothing to do with their hands. Smoking occupies the hands more than one might think until all of the mechanics involved are contemplated. And so what do people do?

To get him over the hump, one fellow picked up a small white stone and kept it in his pocket. Whenever he would begin to feel at loose ends with nothing to do with his hands, he would simply thank the Lord for delivering him from nicotine and rub the smooth white stone in his pocket. Gradually, he had no further need of the crutch and a simple, "Thank you, Lord", relieved the anxiety.

A person who is delivered from a serious problem with lust may suddenly wake up to the fact that he has gradually surrounded himself with people of like perversions. While he needs to pray for his old friends, remaining in the relationships when freshly delivered is like playing with dynamite. He needs to foster relationships with strong Christians who can nurture him until he becomes strong in the Lord.

BE TRANSFORMED BY THE RENEWING OF THE MIND

"Do not conform any longer to the pattern of this world, but be transformed by the renewing of your mind" (Romans 12:2).

Getting into Scripture and seeing what the Word has to say about everything imaginable gets the mind thinking straight. Where demonic influence may have perverted the thinking process, attitudes can be totally changed and thinking processes can be straightened out by immersing oneself in the Word of God.

Putting muscle on the mind through Scripture memorization and meditation protects it from all kinds of mental deterioration. Making it strong through exercising spiritual warfare at the first sign of temptation eliminates untold devastation through weakness.

GET A SLAVE

"I beat my body and make it my slave so that after I have preached to others, I myself will not be disqualified for the prize" (1 Corinthians 9:27).

When a person is being physically demonized, it is not unusual to actually feel the demons screaming in their demands for satisfaction. Gluttony will scream, "Feed me!". Lust will scream, "Give me sex!". The screams reverberate through every cell of the body and it is next to impossible to deny fulfilment.

Once those spirits leave, the screaming demands may be gone, but the habit of caving in to the intense pressures to satisfy the flesh remain as conditioned responses.

The body must be brought under subjection. From a place of mastery over a person, the body must be made the slave.

1Corinthians 3:16 reminds us that our bodies are extremely important to God. *"Don't you know that you yourselves are God's temple and that God's Spirit lives in you? If anyone destroys God's temple, God will destroy him; for God's temple is sacred, and you are that temple."*

Our minds are the caretakers of God's temple.

How would one destroy God's temple? How do we destroy our bodies? - through smoking, drinking, snorting or mainlining toxic substances, through bullemia, anorexia nervosa or gluttony, through ungodly sex etc. etc.

The more we take control of the appetites of our bodies, the fewer problems we have with demonic harassment.

They need to be disciplined with proper rest, balanced nutrition and healthy exercise.

Our bodies are sacred to God. Bringing them into subjection can be a lovely sacrifice of praise.

BE ALERT

Being aware of how the enemy operates and the danger of allowing access through entry points is half of the battle. Satan loves to work through ignorance, but when we are alert to his tactics our danger level is drastically reduced.

Maintaining the full armour of God according to Ephesians 6 is so important.

TAKE CARE OF BUSINESS

At the first suggestion of temptation, take those thoughts captive. If sin enters, deal with it immediately before it gains a foothold and becomes a spiritual problem.

"If we confess our sins, He is faithful and just and will

202

forgive us our sins and purify us from all unrighteousness" (1 John 1:9).

KNOW THE POWER IN PRAISE

"Through Jesus, therefore, let us continually offer to God a sacrifice of praise" (Hebrews 13:15). A Christian who has praise continuously on his or her lips is a victorious Christian.

When we praise God in times of adversity, we communicate trust to Him. Because we are not allowing anything like fear or worry to block His work in our lives, it frees Him to work through the circumstances of our lives.

Besides that, whether we get anything out of it or not, God is worthy of all honour, glory and praise!

FOR FURTHER READING...

Anderson, Neil. *Released from Bondage,*
Here's Life Publishers Inc., 1991

Bagster, Samuel and Sons. *The Zondervan Parallel New Testament in Greek and English.*
The Zondervan Corporation, 1975

Basham, Don. *Deliver us from Evil.*
Fleming H. Revell Company, 1972

Basham, Don and Dick Leggett. *The Most Dangerous Game.* Don W. Basham Publications, 1974

Billheimer, Paul E. *Destined to Overcome.*
Bethany House Publishers, 1982

Billheimer, Paul E. *Destined for the Throne.*
Christian Literature Crusade, 1975

Dake, Finis Jennings. *Dake's Annotated Reference Bible.* Dake Bible Sales,1980

Harrison, Everett F. *Baker's Dictionary of Theology.*
Baker Book House, 1960

Jamieson, Fausset and Brown. *Commentary on the Whole Bible.* Zondervan Publishing House, 1977

Henry, Matthew. *Commentary on the Whole Bible.*
Zondervan Publishing House, 1981

Nee, Watchman. *Spiritual Authority.*
Christian Fellowship Publishers Inc., 1972

Panin, Ivan. *The New Testament from the Greek Text as Established by Bible Numerics.*
The Book Society of Canada, 1966

Philpott, Kent and R.L. Hymers. *The Deliverance Book.* Bible Voice, Inc., 1977

Powell, Graham and Shirley. *Christian Set Yourself Free.* Sovereign World Ltd., 1994

Prince, Derek. *Blessings or Curse - You Can Choose.* Chosen Books, Fleming H. Reve

Putnam, Frank W. *Diagnosis and Treatment of Multiple Personality Disorder.* New York: The Guilford Press, 1989

Roblin Lee, Diane. *Growing in the Spirit.* Praise A V Publishing, 1995

Sanford, John and Mark Sandford. *A Comprehensive Guide to Deliverance and Inner Healing.* Fleming H.Revell, 1992

Sherman, Dean. *Spiritual Warfare for Every Christian.* Crossroads Family of Ministries, YWAM Publishing, 1990

Sherrer, Quinn and Ruthanne Garlock. *A Woman's Guide to Spiritual Warfare.* Servant Publications, 1991

Vine, W.E., M.A. *Vine's Expository Dictionary of Old and New Testament Words.* World Bible Publishers, Iowa Falls

Warren, Bernard. *Illegal Possession.* The Christian Communications Centre, 1987

Webster's New Universal Unabridged Dictionary. New York, Simon and Schuster, 1979

Williams, Janet B.W., text ed. *Diagnostic and Statistical Manual of Mental Disorders.* (3rd ed.) American Psychiatric Association, 1980

MORE PRAISE AV BOOKS AND VIDEOS

Developing Intimacy in Marriage
by Angelo Del Zotto with Diane Roblin Lee
$16.50 Can.-$12.50 U.S.

Quantity.............Total........................

Freedom from Darkness
by Angelo Del Zotto with Diane Roblin Lee
~~$16.50 Can.-$12.50 U.S.~~
18.95   14.85

Quantity.............Total........................

My Father's Child
by Diane Roblin Lee, foreword by Rev. David Mainse
$16.50 Can.-$12.50 U.S.

Quantity.............Total........................

Growing in the Spirit
by Diane Roblin Lee, foreword by Rev. David Mainse
$16.50 Can.-$12.50 U.S.

Quantity.............Total........................

Intimacy in Marriage ~ 9 Session Seminar
by Angelo Del Zotto with Diane Roblin Lee
$179.50 Can.-$135.00 U.S.

Quantity.............Total........................

Video ~ How to Minister Healing and Deliverance
Rev. Angelo and Carmen Del Zotto with Diane Roblin Lee
$29.95 Can.-$19.95 U.S.

Quantity.............Total........................

Video and Colouring Book with Crayons
Bethany Grace and the Little Hooligan
"Just a Few More Minutes" Children's Bedtime Series
$19.95 Can.-$14.00 U.S.

Quantity.............Total........................

	SUB TOTAL........................
Please add appropriate taxes for your residence	Tax #1........................
	Tax #2........................
Postage & handling add $ 3.00 per book or audio	....
$4.00 per video	....
	TOTAL........................

Please check if you would like a catalogue of Praise AV books, videos, audios, plaques and gifts

NAME...
ADDRESS...
CITY......................................PROV./STATE...
COUNTRY .... POSTAL/ZIP.....................................

Please include payment with your order and make cheques payable to:

PRAISE AV PUBLISHING
R.R. #2, WOODVILLE, ONTARIO, CANADA
K0M 2T0
Bookstore discounts available. (705) 439-2751 ~ fax (705) 439-2779